THE BEGINNER'S GUIDE TO

CHICK NIGHT ™

your handbook to HELP and HAPPINESS

COLLEEN KLEVEN

iUniverse, Inc.
Bloomington

The Beginner's Guide to Chick Night™
Your Handbook to Help and Happiness

iUniverse books may be ordered through booksellers or by contacting:

iUniverse
1663 Liberty Drive
Bloomington, IN 47403
www.iuniverse.com
1-800-Authors (1-800-288-4677)

ISBN: 978-1-4620-0501-7 (pbk)
ISBN: 978-1-4620-0502-4 (cloth)
ISBN: 978-1-4620-0503-1 (ebk)

Library of Congress Control Number: 2011905532

Printed in the United States of America

iUniverse rev. date: 7/1/2011

Contents

In the Beginning ...

Conception

This book started out as a gag gift for two girlfriends. In fact, in its original form, there was a list of ten rules for Chick Night and a short explanation of why each one was important. To be honest, I had written that much only because these same two friends had been insisting that I "get the word out to other women" by writing a book about what we were doing.

Right from the start, we called our get-togethers Chick Night, and we referred to ourselves as founding members of the Hanmer chapter of Chick Night. (In case you are unfamiliar with the whereabouts of Hanmer, this small community is located a short twenty-minute drive from Sudbury, Ontario, Canada. In case you're unfamiliar with the whereabouts of Sudbury, the next time you are visiting Toronto, Ontario, Canada, just drive north for four hours. We'll be here waiting.)

Almost instinctively, we made sure these initial Chick Nights always involved chocolate and that they happened once a month. It was this combination that seemed to intrigue every woman we talked to about Chick Night.

Even though our Chick Night get-togethers caused excitement whenever we mentioned them, I still didn't quite understand what all the fuss was about or why my friends thought this was important enough to write a book about. It's not like the idea of female get-togethers was a new concept!

Then I started thinking back to how we had gotten started and how much the three of us had grown as a result of our connection to one another.

That was July 2004. By then, we had been getting together once a month, for chocolate and a few laughs, for more than three years. During that time, we had formed a deep and lasting bond of friendship that none of us had fully anticipated.

Once I started seeing and appreciating what we had created, the book took on a life of its own. By early 2005, I was determined to share my newly developed understanding of the importance of forming a network of female support with as many women as possible. I also realized that to truly explain all the benefits of Chick Night, I would need to call upon the strength, support, and wisdom of other female friends.

Why settle for information from only one source when you can get it from many different sources, right? Throughout the pages of this book, you will hear from each of the founding members of the Hanmer chapter of Chick Night, as well as a number of ladies from a wide range of life circumstances and life stages.

Gestation

You may be asking yourself why this book took six years to complete. To be honest, I let life clutter the path in front of me and stopped taking my own advice: to take time out for me. Before I could get myself refocussed on this book, my entire life derailed.

After twenty-four years of marriage, I suddenly found myself staring down the long road of my future with absolutely no idea what it looked like. With a jolt, I discovered that the picture I had painted for myself—two people sitting together, holding hands and holding grandchildren—was not where I was headed. Only then did I realize that my dream had been based on my grandparents' life and not the life I had actually been living.

So there I was, forty-six years old and feeling like I no longer had an identity.

Whether or not you have faced a moment like this in your life, let me tell you with complete certainty: this is when you will find out who your friends are. I can only hope that you are as fortunate as I was. My circle of friends surrounded me in a group hug that lasted an entire year.

I will never be able to express my gratitude for their love, support, and friendship during that time. However, I can tell you that a truly amazing thing happened. Thanks to their strength, patience, and encouragement, I reconnected with myself. I began to get to know, and like, me.

This may sound like an odd thing to say, but it was during this time that I finally figured out why my friends liked me.

Once the dust settled on this "time of adjustment," I realized I was happier being single than I had been while married. As a result, the relationship between my son and me got even stronger, my friendships (with "the Chicks" and with my other friends, both male and female) became deeper, and my business flourished.

As if those weren't enough positives (and I was truly grateful for each and every one of them!), I began to realize how many dreams and desires I had unconsciously put on hold for many years. That's when I picked up this book again, to a combination of cheers and sighs of relief from "the Chicks." I believe the words most often uttered when I mentioned that I was back to writing this book were "It's about time!"

Labour

I am now more determined than ever to do whatever I can to encourage *you* to develop a circle of friends who will be there when you need them.

There is nothing more therapeutic than sitting with women who truly care about you. They will nurture and coddle you when you need it, and they will give you the proverbial good swift kick in the butt when you need it. The difference with that second part is that they will *not* be kicking you when you are down. True friends will simply tell you the things you need to hear even when—no, especially when—you don't want to hear them.

The best part is that they will tell you these things only out of love, because true friends have no hidden agendas. They are not trying to hurt your feelings or make themselves feel superior. True friends do and say the things that will help you, support you, and cheer you on as you lift yourself up.

The connections you form and the relationships you build through Chick Night are meant to be true and deep and real. They are the key to the success of Chick Night. When you find women who want nothing more than to be a true friend, you will want nothing more than to give them the same in return. The fun and the laughter and the chocolates are bonuses.

These women will help you laugh when you need to, hand you a tissue when a good cry is in order, and encourage, encourage, encourage you to be the absolute best you can be. Tell them your fears and they will help you face them. Tell them your dreams and they will help you reach them.

Delivery

The information, ideas, opinions, and stories in this book are shared in an effort to help you understand the importance of female friendships in your life.

Don't just take my word for it. The ladies who have contributed to this book did so because they want you to experience all the far-reaching benefits of Chick Night.

This book is lovingly dedicated to two very special women: Collette Caza and Bonnie Paquette, the cofounding members of the Hanmer chapter of Chick Night (otherwise known as "two-thirds of the Chicks"). These two wonderful ladies have taught me, while teaching themselves, all the incredible benefits of taking time out for me.

In addition to these founding members, I would also like to acknowledge Tammy Cole, a truly special person who was there before this book began to take shape. I will always be grateful to her for taking a harried housewife and mother under her wing. For three years, she reminded me that I was a person before I was anything else. Thank you, Tammy, for showing me how to have fun again.

I have been extremely fortunate to be surrounded by true friends. They were there when things were going well, they were there during times of crisis, and, more important, they were still there afterward. You will meet some of them in the pages of this book.

My sincere thanks to Laurie Ridler for her unconditional love and friendship, Gynette Cousineau for unwavering support, Dave and Kellie Brown for their exceptional wit and kindness, Louise Bergeron and Dale Boucher for wisdom and insight, and Katherine Huck and Chuck Swindon for sheltering me through the storm.

Many thanks to Karen Campbell, Kate Gravelle, Lisa LaFramboise, Gloria Ann Curwin, Darlene Laferriere, Heather Cartmill, Lynne Raven, Natalie Champagne, Karen Hourtovenko, and Robert Masih. All of you have contributed to my life in your own way. I am grateful for your friendship.

I would like to thank Helen Ghent for more than two decades of mentoring and Sister Bonnie Chesser for her insistence on looking at the truth and living with honour. Both of these women continue to inspire me.

My love and heartfelt thanks to my mother, Joyce Bingham, for her lifelong support and encouragement, her ability to face any challenge with dignity, and her surprising knack for humour and comedic timing. Mom, you never cease to amaze me!

I also wish to express my love and gratitude to Marion and Don Ridler, whom I have always thought of as "Mom and Dad R." Your capacity for kindness is truly appreciated by your "Dot #2."

A lifetime of thanks to my wonderfully spontaneous son, Braedon, who continues to show by his example that no day is too short to cram some fun into. He has provided more than two decades of joy and challenges, frustration and funny stories. Braedon, you are an inspiration to all who know you. I am proud of the man you have become!

Chick Night™ 101: The Concept

Chances are good that you play a number of roles within your extended family: daughter, sister, aunt, wife/ex-wife, mother/stepmom, grandmother.

If you are single (without children) or married (without children), you may still think of yourself as a personal priority—and you may even feel that you have sufficient time to do something about that. Kudos to you if this is where you are in your life! Hold on to that priority and trust the feeling that you have enough time for *you*. Just to be safe, keep this book handy for use as a reference tool when needed.

If you are married and raising children, or a single mother, or a single woman totally committed to her career, or a woman looking after her aging parents, or, or, or ... chances are you have others to do for and you don't have much time to get it all done. You most likely work in and outside the home. On top of putting in all your hours at work, you look after the house and everyone in the house, doing the cooking, cleaning, laundry, and groceries, helping with homework, running errands, driving "Mom's Taxi," and so on, and so on, and so on!

Even if you are single and without children, you spend the majority of your waking hours tending to the demands of your job, your boss, your supervisor, your coworkers, and your clients. You have short-term deadlines and long-term goals that can consume most of your time and energy if you let them.

Regardless of marital status and whether or not you have children, you may also be dealing with any number of other complexities and challenges, including looking after aging parents, or providing assistance to members of your extended family, or being there for your friends, or, or ...

You can see where I'm going with this. Your time is in high demand, but I'll bet you are doing the best you can to make sure that everything gets done and everyone is taken care of. Or are you?

You may be forgetting to take care of the most important person in your life—*you*!

At this point, you are probably rolling your eyes skyward and thinking, "What is she talking about? I take care of me! I eat when I can, get as much sleep as my schedule will allow, and after working and chasing kids around all day, I certainly get enough exercise to do me some good!"

Just let me ask you this one simple question: when was the last time you went out with the girls? (Taking your daughter to get new running shoes or taking your coffee break with female coworkers doesn't count.)

I'm asking you again: when was the last time you went out for an adults-only evening with one or more of your women friends?

If you can't answer that question without checking the calendar on the wall in your kitchen, flipping through the day planner on your desk, or calling up your computerized calendar, the Chick Night concept is long overdue for you.

Come Out, Come Out, Wherever You Are!

Before we delve into the nitty-gritty of the how, when, and where of the successful operation of Chick Night, it is imperative that you understand *why* this practice is so important. The sad truth is that somewhere along the way, we women forget about ourselves. We forget how to have fun, we forget how to recharge our batteries, and we forget the importance of spending time with girlfriends. We simply forget!

It happens while we're not looking. It happens as our lives begin to fill up with the time-consuming activities, commitments, and responsibilities on our individual lists. How many of these apply to you: boyfriend, husband, children, career, extended family, friends, community, faith group, volunteer obligations?

All these demands on our time mean that something, or someone, has to fall off the list. It seems to be almost universal that when something needs to be eliminated to "save time," we choose to eliminate ourselves from our list of priorities.

Okay, I can hear a few of you exclaiming indignantly, "I do not!" Well, perhaps you haven't actually eliminated yourself, but before you demand a formal apology, I challenge you to take a good look at *where* you are on the list. Are you in the top three? Are you even in the top five? Or are you somewhere down on page two, sandwiched between picking up batteries for the smoke detector and sorting out all that junk in the garage?

Would you like to take a wild guess as to how I knew what questions to ask you?

Yes—I did the same thing to myself. After homeschooling my son for his grade three year, I had taken a full-time contract in the copy department at a local radio station. I spent my days writing commercials and fielding calls from my son's principal (while he tried to adjust to sitting still in a classroom with twenty-six other kids.) Evenings and weekends were spent doing all the groceries, cooking, cleaning, and laundry necessary to run a household.

My wake-up call came during a phone conversation with a twentysomething coworker. Nat asked me the last time I'd gone out on a Saturday night. It was an innocent question, but when I grabbed my calendar, I was flabbergasted to discover that I had to go back eleven months to answer her. At that moment, I felt 150 years old, when in reality, I wasn't quite forty.

Shortly after that, I was fortunate enough to meet a woman who took one look at what I was doing to myself and said, "When did you stop being worthy?" Tammy firmly announced her intention to reintroduce me to the concept of having fun. It was such a simple statement that, at the time, I didn't fully understand the effect her gift would have on my life.

They say, "When the student is ready, the teacher will appear." That was certainly the case for me. Tammy was an excellent teacher. Under her expert tutelage, we spent more than a year having spontaneous and hilarious "Chick time" together.

By the time her career took her to another part of the country, her inspiration had awakened the section of my brain that stored the concept of having fun.

I now gladly pass along that favour by sharing this wisdom with you …

The Birth of Chick Night™

After Tammy moved away, I discovered how much I missed having fun with another woman. At the time, I was in a house where even the dog and two budgies were male. I felt slightly outnumbered: Testosterone 5, Estrogen 1. Female fellowship was a must!

Armed with what I had learned about "Chick time," I called two girlfriends, Bonnie and Collette, and asked them if they wanted to go out for a girls-only evening.

"You mean … just us?" they asked. I said, "Yeah. No kids, no husbands, just us." When I suggested we go out for the chocolate dessert of their choice, they quickly agreed.

Chick Night began as a tasty quest for the best chocolate dessert within a fifty-kilometre radius. As undeniably enjoyable as these culinary treasure hunts were, it soon became apparent to all three of us that our "night out with the girls" was evolving into a quest for something greater.

I wish I could tell you the exact date and time of the birth of Chick Night. It would be great fun for we three founding members of the Hanmer chapter (named after the town in which we live) of Chick Night to be able to celebrate the occasion on a yearly basis. (Hey, what am I thinking? We celebrate Chick Night on a *monthly* basis! Muuuch better!)

Chick Night™: The Gift You Give Yourself

Because I am the logistical coordinator of the Hanmer chapter of Chick Night, the task of organizing the time and place falls to me. I usually start the ball rolling by e-mailing suggestions several weeks in advance. This may strike you as too complicated or time consuming for your busy schedule, but I implore you to give it some thought before you dismiss the idea. Instead of throwing up all sorts of barriers (lack of time, lack of money), call one or two close girlfriends and, using this handbook, set up a date.

The following pages will help you get acquainted with some of the guidelines—known as the Ten to Remember—that Bonnie, Collette, and I have discovered are essential elements of Chick Night. These essentials are the result of several years of "research" and groundwork, as we lovingly tried and tested concepts for the benefit of future chapters of Chick Night. (In the case of Rule #1, I admit that we have done a lot of testing.)

I am passing along the rules, and the reasoning behind the rules, in the hope that you will become a founding member of your very own official or unofficial chapter of Chick Night. Once you start to incorporate Chick Night into your life—and I sincerely hope that you do—you will begin to discover the incredible benefits of putting yourself back on your priority list.

Chick Night™ Rule #1:
All Chick Nights™ Must
Involve Chocolate

(also known as our "I Love Rules" rule)

The rule that all Chick Nights must involve chocolate instantly became a "must" for us. It is not necessary to make chocolate the focal point of your evening, but it is sure to be one of the highlights. Chocolate serves as a reminder that you *deserve* to be treated. A little bit of chocolate can go a long way toward making a woman feel pampered.

Observance of this most sacred practice can take the form of a box of chocolates, a chocolate fondue, a "treasure hunt" search of all restaurants, cafés, bakeries, and dessert bars in your area (in an attempt to discover the best dessert spot), or simply the consumption of one deliciously luxurious mug of hot chocolate. The choice (as with all Chick Night activities) is yours.

For those unfortunate souls who are either allergic to or (heaven forbid!) don't like chocolate, your options are still open. Perhaps caramels, gummy bears, or hard candies will do the trick. Restaurants, dessert bars, and confectioner's shops are loaded with tasty and effective alternatives. Choose a substitute that delivers a comparable sense of pleasure. It's that delicious sense of indulgence that you're after.

For those of you who are constantly dieting, currently dieting, planning on dieting, or dreading a diet, I urge you to read the following excerpt from the Hanmer chapter of Chick Night regulations Section C (for Chocolate), Subsection 2B:

> After careful consideration and thoughtful discussion by all three founding members, the vote is unanimous: chocolate (in any form) consumed during the normal course of any and all Chick Nights is, now and forever, deemed calorie-free and fat-free.

As you can see, our founding members wisely chose to abolish all calorie counting, worry, or guilt normally associated with the consumption of chocolate. Right from the start, we wanted Chick Night to be fun! As various issues cropped up, we began to compile an unofficial list of "regulations" we could quote from when a to-heck-with-it attitude was called for. These regulations became our way of enjoying a little guilt-free pleasure during Chick time (see Rule #8). It is denial lived in its most sublime form.

I will share more excerpts from the Hanmer chapter of Chick Night regulations with you throughout this book. Feel free to borrow them or write your own if you wish. Use whatever you think will work for you.

Once you have put your own personal touches on Chick Night, I would *love* to hear from you. Tell me your stories! I'm an avid reader and a great listener. Share girlfriends, share!

The Universal Language of Chocolate

It is common knowledge within the medical community (and among chocolate lovers) that eating chocolate stimulates the production of endorphins, which create feelings of pleasure, and raises the levels of serotonin, which acts as an antidepressant. It should come as no surprise that most of us associate chocolate with pleasant thoughts and memories.

Chocolate, that sweet and mouthwatering nectar of the goddesses, speaks to each of us in different ways. When I use the word *speaks*, I mean it quite literally. Chocolate has a voice of its own. It calls us, beckons us, with promises of tasty pleasure. Chocolate can create a quiet moment in an otherwise hectic lifestyle. It has the power to mark the end of a horrendous day and help you begin the process of physical, mental, and emotional relaxation.

Chocolate has been in existence since the days of the Central American Mayan culture. More than two thousand years ago, the Mayans began to crush cocoa beans into a powder to drink as a dark chocolate beverage that they believed had certain spiritual properties. The Aztecs also drank the unsweetened liquid during their sacred ceremonies.

Christopher Columbus brought cocoa beans back to Spain in 1502, but it wasn't until the Spanish explorer Hernando Cortez arrived in Mexico in 1519 that anyone realized that *chocolatl* (its original Aztec name) could be sweetened with cane sugar and marketed.

Thankfully, solid eating chocolate was invented in 1847. Milk chocolate was created less than thirty years later.

I mean it when I say "thankfully," because chocolate really can work wonders. It can work for you, or you can pass on the magic to someone else. A box of chocolates can be a simple yet powerful statement that allows the giver to express an emotional connection with the recipient. It can say, "I love you." It can say, "I was thinking about you." Or it can simply say, "I noticed you're having a rough day. Hope this helps."

Even a single chocolate, beautifully wrapped and presented to someone you care about, will be appreciated and enjoyed for the little taste of heaven that it offers. That moment of bliss may be just the thing that gets your friend through a difficult time. By keeping a few individually wrapped chocolates tucked away in your freezer, you will always be ready. Think of these chocolates as the "in case of emergency, break glass" type of gift. If you doubt me, try giving a single piece of chocolate to someone who is not expecting it. Pay attention to the emotional reaction you get.

In addition to the spiritual, psychological, and emotional benefits that have been attributed to chocolate since those early Mayan civilizations, there are physiological benefits that scientists are just now recognizing. More and more studies are being done, with findings all pointing to some important facts. The flavonoid content in the cocoa bean has antioxidant properties—the same properties that give berries, red wine, and green tea their health benefits. The darker and more unrefined the chocolate, the more flavonoids it retains.

I'm not making this up. The *American Journal of Clinical Nutrition* published a study in their March 2007 issue linking the consumption of flavonoid-rich food with a lower risk of developing coronary heart disease. In this same report, chocolate was ranked as one of the top flavonoid-rich foods (right up there with bran, red wine, grapefruit, and strawberries). Other studies, including one published in the *Journal of the American Medical Association*, have linked the daily consumption of small portions of dark chocolate to a reduction in blood pressure.

It is perfectly understandable that chocolate elicits our exuberant and "heartfelt" response!

Nectar of the Goddesses

No wonder chocolate is present at most major events. Chances are, your first birthday cake was chocolate. Valentine's Day gifts include chocolate. The Easter Bunny brings chocolate. All of these occasions are opportunities for chocolate to represent joy, happiness, pleasure, and love. Is it any wonder that the founding members of Chick Night immediately incorporated chocolate into the regulations?

Looking back, I really can't remember a time in my life when I didn't love chocolate. Chocolate has always been there, willing to help me celebrate in the good times and cheer me up when I've been sad. It is truly the nectar of the goddesses.

There is one specific time of the month when my personal chocolate craving takes on monumental urgency. I'm talking about the-house-is-on-fire-and-a-tornado-is-headed-this-way-but-they-will-both-have-to-WAIT-while-I-eat-this-piece-of-chocolate kind of craving.

I still clearly remember finding myself stuck inside during a winter blizzard that had closed schools, office buildings, and stores, and had crippled bus transit, about twenty-five years ago. On this most inopportune of days, I discovered that I didn't have any chocolate in the apartment. My craving got so bad that I put together a pan of chocolate brownies and stuck them in the oven to bake. Twenty minutes later, I was sitting cross-legged on the floor in front of the stove. When asked what on earth I was doing, I very matter-of-factly replied, "Waiting."

Now that I think back on it, I realize that all the great spiritual leaders of the past have spoken of the virtue of patience. If only they had thought to teach this concept using chocolate!

I learned something valuable that day. I learned to always be prepared. Ever since my brownies incident, I have kept a chocolate stash hidden somewhere in the house. My son takes great delight in finding "Mom's stash." It has become a game for us over the years. Once he has announced the secret location of Mom's stash, it is time for me to hide it in a new spot. He never actually touches my hidden cache of chocolate. Finding it simply signals the start of a new game.

I had always thought that I was the only woman who did this, but it turns out that hiding chocolate is a hereditary trait. About fifteen years ago, I was teasing my mom about all the stuff she keeps in her downstairs freezer. (My mom has a habit of piling new food on top of the old stuff, so you never know how long the hamburger at the bottom of the freezer has been there.) I made a joking reference to all the meat loaf she used to have in that downstairs freezer when we were kids. Mom burst out laughing and said, "Didn't you ever figure it out?" She then admitted that when we were little, she used to buy three family-size Cadbury Burnt Almond dark chocolate bars. She would wrap the stack of them in tin foil and store them in the downstairs freezer. After she had put us to bed, she could sit down in peace and quiet to enjoy a few sections of her favourite chocolate bar. Whenever one of us would spot these secret tin-foil-wrapped stashes and ask what was inside, she would say, "Oh, that? It's just leftover meat loaf." It guaranteed that none of us would explore any further. (I told you this was hereditary!)

When I asked my mom what chocolate means to her, this was her response:

What Chocolate Means to Me

by Joyce Bingham

CHOCOLATE, mmmmmmmm good. I love the smell of chocolate and the taste of chocolate. I frequently choose desserts made of chocolate. Nanaimo bars, chocolate squares, and hot chocolate (but never chocolate ice cream). I prefer solid chocolate rather than the kind with sticky sweet fillings. Of course, liqueur-filled chocolates are acceptable. Chocolate-covered nuts are delicious too.

I often use chocolate as a reward. When I have to do a distasteful/

boring/unpleasant job, such as writing report cards or essays or doing housework (cleaning, washing floors), I set myself a task and then a reward. For example: write three report cards and then have ONE square of chocolate.

Years ago, too much chocolate gave me a headache, so I couldn't eat a lot at once. Since I had to write anywhere from forty-five to sixty-three kindergarten report cards for each term, I had to ration out the chocolate or I would have had a raging headache and not felt well enough to write the reports. I probably also would not have had the patience to say what I meant in a nonoffensive manner.

I never have to reward myself when I work in the garden. That is never a chore. However, sometimes I am tired after several hours of gardening and never refuse a treat!

When your aunt Doris and I were in South Korea to visit your brother, David, he brought some hot chocolate from McDonald's to our hotel room. I don't think anything has ever tasted so good. We were both tired, and all the Korean food was spicy and strange. Your brother had to leave our hotel, climb up a number of steps to a bridge, cross over a twelve-lane road above street level, and then go down the steps on the other side to reach McDonald's. McDonald's was on the second floor of the restaurant. Then he had to climb up all those stairs again, cross the bridge above the traffic, and go down the steps on the other side to reach our hotel. I can't speak for him, but I know your aunt and I thought it was well worth the effort!

On a different trip, I purchased some chocolate in the airports in Amsterdam and Switzerland. They all have slightly different flavours. ALL are delicious.

I purchased a chocolate fondue set before Christmas at Laura Secord's, but we didn't have time to try it. Next time you come we will dip some banana slices and strawberries in chocolate. Yum!

I LOVE the way my mom thinks!

Actually, I love my mom, period—which brings up an important point I would like to make. Throughout the pages of this book, we will look at the importance of forming friendships and nurturing these beneficial relationships with women. While you are seeking out these women, you might want to pay attention to the fact that even though your mother is your mom, she is also a woman.

I have had many wonderful times with my Chick Night Chicks (and you will read about a lot of those times in the following pages). I have also had wonderful times sitting and drinking tea and talking to my mom.

If you love and trust your mother, don't discount her as a potential Chick—even if those get-togethers are always one-on-one Chick times. Few bonds you ever develop will be as close and as deep as the one you have (or can have) with her.

Cherish and nurture the relationship with this woman in your life. If you are as fortunate as I have been, your mom is one of the special people in the world who truly has your best interests at heart.

Another Chapter on Chocolate: A Chick Night™ Guiding Principle

Let's check in with the other two founding members of the Hanmer chapter of Chick Night and find out what they have to say on the sweet subject of chocolate.

What Chocolate Means to Me

by Bonnie Paquette

I admit it! I call myself a chocoholic. I LOVE chocolate. I ADORE chocolate (especially dark chocolate dipped in hot tea). How did chocolate become such an obsession with me? To tell you the truth, it wasn't always like this. In fact, when I was growing up, I NEVER ate chocolate. (Well, not exactly.) I ate chocolate, but it was only white. To me, white chocolate is not *real* chocolate. The reason for my abstinence wasn't dislike or denial. I was simply allergic to it.

The worst time of year for me was Easter. I remember my sister getting all the "good" chocolate (luscious dark or creamy milk chocolate) while I received a nontraditional white bunny. I tried to pretend mine was brown, but it didn't work. I still yearned for the taste of dark chocolate.

By the time I reached puberty, a magnificent thing had happened. (No, not that ...) I had grown OUT of my allergy to chocolate. The ban was lifted! No more white bunnies for ME!

I have a lot of catching up to do. To be able to enjoy REAL chocolate at Easter, or Valentine's, or the second Tuesday of the month, or ... is my absolute sweetest delight. To be able to enjoy it in the company of my Chick friends on Chick Nights is even better!

Outgrowing an allergy to chocolate. Isn't that the most heartwarming happy ending you've ever heard?! Here's what Collette had to say on this subject:

The Wonderful World of Chocolate

by Collette Caza

My fascination with chocolate began when I discovered Chick Night. You see, I would have said I love spinach just to belong to this elite group of women who have invented their own form of the Ya-Ya Sisterhood club.

Only recently have I given any real thought to chocolate. Now that I have considered the subject for a while, I have come up with my own theory as to why chocolate and Chick time go together.

I've always thought of chocolate as being associated with the Easter season and the "bunny" that comes hopping by your house to bring your special treat of Easter chocolate.

I come from a family of four children. Anyone from a big family will see the problem immediately: 4 hyper children + Easter chocolate + limited space = 1 frazzled mom. Not good math no matter how you look at it!

When I was a child, the bunny would bring a single chocolate egg with each child's name on it. My mom then stood a fighting chance of keeping ahead of a house full of hyper youngsters.

See if you can follow my theory. The chocolate egg of my childhood gave birth to a Chick. Therefore, the Chick came from the chocolate egg. Since Chick and chocolate are so obviously a match ... then Chick + chocolate = Chick Night!

When we Chicks begin to share (and reality occasionally gets to be too much), a shot of chocolate always does the trick. After any necessary (yet sometimes painful) injection of truth, we wash it down with chocolate. As Julie Andrews so aptly put it during a classic moment in the movie *Mary Poppins,* it helps the medicine go down.

So here's to chocolate, or spinach, or whatever it takes to get YOU out of the house once in a while.

Just for the record, I am absolutely positive that the Geneva Conventions strictly prohibit the use of spinach as a substitute for chocolate "for humanitarian reasons."

Last, but certainly not least, this is what my dear mentor Tammy (the Tinker Bell of Fun and Frivolity, the patron saint of Chick Night) had to say when I asked her:

What Chocolate Means to Me

by Tammy Cole

It's not every day you get to have a writing "assignment" about your first love ... chocolate. I have a very good memory and truly believe I have a whole file cabinet in my brain that stores my fondest chocolate memories.

The love affair began when my older sister started kindergarten. Once she was out of the house, it was my time with Mom. She had an old, green, men's ten-speed bike with a metal child carrier on the back, and the two of us would bike to the corner store for a treat ... a treat that always had a chocolate connection, with jujubes, ice cream, Popsicles, even soda—all chocolate flavoured!

It was our ritual. It was our secret. My older sister never knew of our escapades, and the tradition was never passed along to my younger sister. It was my special bonding time with my mom. Over the years, chocolate and the indulgence that goes along with it has been the sweet part of the glue that bonds me to my favourite people.

I love the way Chick Night brought Colleen and me together. I remember countless nights at Colleen's house with big bags of chocolate. We would pretend that there was no way we could ever eat it all. HA! It would disappear between chats about work, favourite shows, hopes, ambitions, and fears. Some of those tasty morsels were the only other witnesses when we shared things that we never imagined would be placed in someone else's trust.

It's when I think back on those nights that I see the parallels between chocolate and friendship. Milk chocolate is that warm hug a friend gives you whether you deserve it or not. Dark chocolate is rich with a little bite like a true friend who tells you what you need to hear instead of what you want to hear. White chocolate is what we're all striving for in friendship ... not perfection, but purity.

I live too far away now to attend Hanmer Chick Night, but when I think of Colleen, I'll wander over to my stash of chocolate. You see, most of my chocolate is a gift from her. Each piece is a reminder of our connection. Normally, chocolate in my house doesn't last very long ... but this stuff is for special occasions ...

Isn't it remarkable how chocolate can trigger memories and emotional connections? From its earliest form, the drinking chocolate used in Mayan ceremonies and rituals, to the delectable selection of chocolate confectionery available today, there has always been something mysterious and special about the way chocolate affects people. This isn't just a tasty treat—it's a bonding tool.

Chick Night™ Rule #2: Chick Night™ Must Happen a Minimum of Once a Month

---

(Pay attention to yourself at least as often as you pay attention to your utility bills.)

This one is mandatory! You cannot let Chick Night get lost in the shuffle of your life. It must take place at least once a month. I cannot stress the importance of this point strongly enough. Start off gently. Arrange for one evening a month that is just for you. Don't talk yourself out of doing it. Start putting yourself first. If you don't … who will?!

The logic behind planning your Chick Night schedule is twofold. First, these Chick Nights are meant to help you rediscover how critical time for yourself really is. If Chick Night happens only sporadically, or (even worse) as a one-shot deal, you will never reap the emotional and psychological (that's shop talk for *morale*) benefits of Chick Night.

The second (more practical) reason for booking Chick Night well in advance is that women *do* have busy schedules. Trying to coordinate with three or more women is often easier said than done. Our chapter has opted for Saturday night Chick Night. However, your group should not limit yourselves to this one particular night of the week. There is no special significance to Saturday. It simply works best for us.

When you and two or three or more of your girlfriends have formed your very own chapter of Chick Night, I highly recommend that you choose a logistical coordinator. She will call or e-mail all members ahead of time to book future Chick Nights well in advance.

In our case, I am logistical coordinator. I take my role seriously. I have been known to organize the date and time of next month's meeting while we were on our way home from this month's Chick Night. The few times I wasn't nearly this quick on the draw, my fellow Chicks have cheerfully picked up the slack.

Once your group has engaged in several successful Chick Nights, it will become easier to set aside the time. However, in the event that an entire calendar month seems to be slipping away without the possibility of snagging even one evening that works for everyone in your group … you can use this little-known provision in the Hanmer chapter of Chick Night regulations Section D, Subsection 3A, which clearly states the following:

> All authorized chapters of Chick Night have the right to reassign, reposition, or recategorize specific calendar dates for the purpose of celebrating Chick Night.

In other words, ladies, don't let something as simple as the arrival of a new calendar month interfere with your Chick Night fun. Simply exercise your creative thinking and turn April 3 into March 34.

Laugh if you want (and I encourage you to laugh as often as you can!), but this scenario also provides a wonderful opportunity for you to create a new habit: doing something *you* would like to do.

Contrary to popular misconception, going out for Chick Night once a month is *not* a selfish or rebellious act. It is simply about putting yourself back on the list and offering yourself the same consideration you offer everyone else.

How often do you make every possible effort to be flexible and accommodating with your schedule so that someone else can do what *he or she* wants? I'm talking about rearranging your schedule so you can handle a client's last-minute request or run an errand for a friend or family member or drive your kids to [fill in one of the three most frequent Mom's Taxi's destinations]. I am also referring to times when you have made alternative arrangements to get to work or wherever you needed to go so someone else could use your vehicle.

Do you consider it selfish for someone to ask you for a ride? Is asking to borrow your car a selfish thing for a family member to do? If you don't consider these selfish requests, then on some level you must acknowledge that *doing* them for people is an act of *thoughtfulness on your part.*

Isn't it about time you showed yourself the same thoughtfulness? Instead of automatically accepting that getting together with friends "isn't going to work this month," figure out a way that it will. Then make plans to go out.

I've been doing all the talking about Rule #2. If you still aren't quite convinced that you deserve Chick Night on a regular monthly basis, I will let my two cofounders have a whirl.

What Chick Night™ Means to Me

by Collette Caza

Chick time allows me the opportunity to be completely real. In doing so, I have made a remarkable discovery. When I take time to hang around with vibrant, alive women who are not afraid to be themselves, I am able to feel free to be me. The process works pretty much like osmosis.

As I share laughter and tears, Chick Night brings me closer to my friends. I know that through Chick time, I have found two bosom (pun intended) buddies. What surprised me is that I also found another one. I found the "me" that was hidden deep down inside, buried beneath a mountain of dirty laundry, expectations, and demands on my time.

I also found out that I can belong to an elite group of individuals— none of whom I married or gave birth to. I can like who I am. I can be open and vulnerable in the company of other women. Time and time again, I discover that the problems, worries, and concerns I am facing are also being faced by my Chick friends.

I have discovered that when you start to like who you are, it becomes easier to love others. After a night out with the Chicks, I come back a better person. Not only do I get the benefits, but so does my family.

So, for all you men out there ... hey, what are you doing reading this book? (Just kidding.) For all you men out there, encourage your wife or girlfriend to have her own Chick time at least once a month. Trust me, you'll be glad you did.

Now it's Bonnie's turn:

What Chick Night™ Means to Me

by Bonnie Paquette

Chick Night is one of those special things in my life that I didn't plan for, but now that it *is* part of my life, I wonder how I ever managed without it! I was introduced to Chick Night at a time when I really needed something just for me. I was a single mom and working full time. Special time set aside for me hardly existed. No, that's a lie. Special time for me did *not* exist. On those extremely rare occasions when I actually had time for myself, I didn't go anywhere. All of my extended family lives out of town. Most of my friends were married. I didn't want to take precious time away from them (and their families), especially on weekends. Saturday nights were typically spent doing my ironing while watching a movie on TV.

Then one day, out of the blue (or so it seemed at the time), the first Chick Night was hatched. Before I knew it, Chick Night was a monthly Saturday routine.

It gave me something to look forward to. It gave me a special outing. It got me out of the house. It became a gift I gave to myself.

Guess what?! My ironing still manages to get done!

Let me just add a small tip: nothing you own that can be thrown into your dryer (along with a clean, damp washcloth) for five minutes ever needs to get ironed again. Ironing, shmironing!

Women never seem to forget the jobs still waiting for them on the home front. I'm really hoping that this book will help you start remembering to put *yourself* ahead of errands, floors, dishes, and ironing.

Countdown to Chick Night™:
26 More Sleeps … 25 … 24 … 23 …

You have now heard why having Chick Night once a month is important to Collette and Bonnie. The best way I can explain its importance to me is by telling you about the incident that taught me this lesson.

It happened more than a dozen years ago. It didn't seem very funny at the time, but I laugh about it now. In fact, it's become one of my favourite stories highlighting the trials and tribulations of raising my son. By the way, if you do not yet have children, don't worry. No child of *yours* will ever do anything like this.

Footprints in the Sanding

Any woman who has been a mother for more than ten days has a story to tell. We have all experienced moments when, despite our very real love for our child, we have wondered, "What the heck was I thinking?" when we decided to start a family. The older your children get, the longer your list of stories will be.

Of all my possible examples of a time when Chick Night came to my rescue, this one stands out from the others. It beats the fact that my son, Braedon, started walking at ten months and running a mere one week later. (Ask my mother—she is my witness!) It tops the time he rode his three-wheel motorcycle right off the top landing, sailed straight out over five stairs, and collided with the front door (at five feet off the ground). It even outranks the time he discovered that jumping out his bedroom window (a nine-foot drop) was a much more efficient route to the backyard than walking all the way around the outside of the house. Each of these events occurred *before* my son was four years old. Are you starting to get a picture of my life back then?

Fast-forward six years to a crisp fall afternoon when Braedon was ten years old. The previous weekend had been spent installing a tongue-and-groove pine floor in the master bedroom. I was now finishing the sanding and applying three coats of industrial-grade polyurethane.

All went well until I applied the second coat.

Fumes from the polyurethane I was using are extremely strong. I was purposely taking a nice long walk between coats to clear my head and allow most of the fumes to escape through the open bedroom window. Unfortunately, while I was gone, my son arrived home from school. We had a policy that, in the event that Mommy wasn't home and the front door was locked, he was to go across the street to my friend and neighbour Jan's house and wait there.

I will never figure out why, on this of all days, he decided not to go to Jan's house. Instead, he went around to the back of our shed, grabbed a ten-foot ladder, leaned it up against the back of the house, and crawled through the only window that was open.

Yes, my darling child jumped through the master bedroom window and proceeded to walk across that freshly polyurethaned floor wearing his winter boots. He was within two feet of the doorway when he suddenly realized what he was doing. He panicked, turned around, and walked all the way back to the window. He was climbing back outside when I arrived.

I don't need to describe the condition of the floor between the window and the doorway. I'm sure I don't need to tell you my emotional response to it, either. Let's just say that my son and I will always be grateful for the ten feet of floor that separated us at that exact moment.

They say timing is everything. Sometimes timing can work against you (in the case of my walk during my son's arrival home from school). Sometimes timing can be absolutely perfect. In this case, Tammy, my fun and frivolity mentor, had *perfect* timing. She called just as I was inhaling that huge lungful of oxygen necessary to start blasting away at a child who is about to get seriously told off. Braedon climbed down the ladder into our backyard as I began to tell Tammy what he had just done. Not having any children of her own, but certainly in possession of a brain, Tammy immediately comprehended the seriousness of the situation. Within ten minutes, she had arrived at my door with enough chocolate to impress a 911 paramedic.

Tammy filled my bathtub with bubble bath and hot water, handed me all that chocolate, shoved me into the bathroom, and shut the door. I spent the next thirty minutes soaking, munching, and calming down while Tammy helped my son do his homework at the kitchen table.

When I look back on this incident, I always marvel that this episode had anything even remotely resembling a happy ending. Without Tammy's quick thinking and equally quick arrival, that evening would have been an unhappy few hours. I would have been feeling angry and frustrated, and Braedon would have been banished to his bedroom and told to "think about what you've done." The only reason it ended on a sweet note is because of the timely intervention of a Chick.

I can't promise you that your Chick Night network of friends will always have the kind of radar antennae that Tammy proved to have that fateful day. However, I can assure you that knowing you can count on adult female companionship at least one evening a month will go a long way toward helping you cope with the many challenges that like to pop up in life.

When you have Chick Night to look forward to, it can be your light at the end of a long and trying month. It can help you maintain your balance, keep your perspective, and hold on to your sanity during times when you're actually afraid to wonder what else could go wrong.

Re: "Footprints in the Sanding": My son is much older and slightly less impetuous now, plus he doesn't know where you live, so you should be okay. However, if you ever encounter a similar situation, here's what to do: *Lightly sand the affected area. Mix two parts polyurethane with one part mineral spirits. Use this mixture on the affected area only. Allow to dry overnight. The next day, resume applying fresh coats of polyurethane (as if nothing happened) to the entire floor.*

The Observations of an Offspring

It has been more than a decade since that incident with the floor. I can laugh about it now. In fact, Braedon and I use it as our favourite example of how Chick Night can come to the rescue of even the most impetuous of offspring. Over the years, I've watched my son grow up into a really terrific young man. He's funny, outgoing, caring, compassionate ... and very observant. I asked Braedon to talk about Chick Night from his perspective as the son of a Chick.

How Chick Night™ Has Benefitted My Mom

by Braedon Kleven

My mom has been doing Chick Night since I was a kid. First it was with Tammy, and then when Tammy moved away, my mom started getting together with Bonnie and Collette. Chick Night has been a social network builder and a friendship builder for my mom because it's a guaranteed once-a-month thing. I know it means a lot to her because when Chick Night comes up in conversation, her eyes light up and true excitement rises from within her.

All other plans and tickets to shows can be cancelled or missed out on, but not Chick Night. It is one of the biggest events of the month, and for good reason. In ten years, I have never heard her say, "Chick Night sucked tonight," because if they saw a crappy movie at least they got to see it together.

My mom is happier because of Chick Night. I think the number one reason for that is because she has people she can confide in other than family members. Sometimes family isn't as objective as your close friends.

Having a Chick Night with Collette and Bonnie means that she will have hours of heart-to-heart conversations about everything. These are guaranteed, intense sessions of bonding that my mom looks forward to. I think she feels freer now because she has these ladies who she can talk to about anything.

I know that the confidentiality between them is strong and important.

Whatever they talk about never leaves the group. How could you stay close friends for ten years if you had a backstabber in the group? Think about it.

These women are so good to each other. They talk about their feelings, they laugh, they cry, they vent, and it all helps. Instead of a book-smart thing, it's based on having lived life and understanding what the other woman is going through.

Chick Night is like a psychiatrist session—with chocolate.

The Voice of Experience

Just to prove that Bonnie, Collette, and I are not the only women in the world who think you deserve Chick Night, I would like to give you the opportunity to hear from Bonnie's mother, Betty. When Bonnie told her mom that I was writing a book about our shared experiences, she sat down and wrote me a lovely letter explaining how she and a group of her friends were handling retirement.

The RODEO (Retired Old Dames Eating Out) Gals

by Betty Blair Smith

We began our group with four retired teachers who had all taught special-needs children (those with mental, physical, and emotional challenges). As teachers, we had supported one another by sharing our problems and our successes. Over the years, we had shared a few tears and many smiles. We were confidantes for each other. When we retired, we missed that close relationship.

After several years of retirement, we decided it was time to get together again. Our friend Jean knew about the ROMEO Boys (Retired Old Men Eating Out), and she thought we should be the RODEO Gals. We all agreed.

It is amazing how busy four retired ladies had become! Like most retirees, our days were filled with appointments, volunteer work, church work, housework, social events, and (of course) grandchildren. Sometimes we wonder how we ever had time to work!

After many phone calls, a time and place was finally arranged. We met for lunch and conversation. The conversation was the most important part. When you put four retired teachers together, there is always lots of conversation! We have memories to share and important news to catch up on. My husband always asked, "What do you find to talk about?" We just never run out of conversation.

We have so many laughs. Our time together lifts our spirits. Each time we meet, we set the date for the next luncheon, which is usually every other month. As we are growing older, it becomes more difficult. One of us has had a hip replacement, another has had eye surgery.

Our initial group has grown. When Dorothy retired two years ago, she joined the RODEO Gals. She had worked with us for many years and has become a genuine member of our little group.

It is so important to touch base with each other. We need the time together. After so many years of friendship, we know we are in "safe" company. Our confidences will be always be respected.

There really are "no friends like old friends." Old friends know your faults and still care about you. They are true friends and precious treasures.

I salute these ladies for creating their own version of Chick Night. It works for them—and that works for me! Congratulations, ladies.

Chick Night™ Rule #3:
No Children Allowed

(It's okay to like this rule!)

Under *no* circumstances should any woman bring her children to Chick Night. The evening cannot, and will not, be a Chick Night if even one member has to play her "mom" role.

This includes offspring of all ages (even teenage daughters). No matter how "quiet" your young ones will be, or how much "fun" your older ones might be to have around, the answer still needs to be no.

Your children may resort to begging, temper tantrums, guilt trips, and any combination of manipulative tricks they can think of to try to be included in your evening. Be strong! Do not cave in! Remember, this is *your* evening. (And how many of those do you actually get?!)

If your children continue to beg to come along (and they will when they start hearing how much fun you are having), you can cite the following bylaw from the Hanmer chapter of Chick Night, regulations Section N, Subsection O:

> No offspring of any member may attend a Chick Night. N-O spells "NO"!

This regulation is short, sweet, and to the point.

Holding firm to this rule also applies to possible manipulation from adult members of your group who may try to bring their children with them. As mothers, we are all aware that unforeseen circumstances can sometimes wreak havoc with our best-laid plans. Babysitters cancel at the last minute, ex-husbands reschedule their weekends, and so on.

In the event that a Chick Night member discovers she has absolutely no one to watch her children, she may *not* bring them along. Instead, combine your Chick Night resources to come up with a solution that works. Perhaps one member has teenagers who can babysit the younger children of another member, or perhaps you can recommend a different babysitter.

The key here is *networking*. Ladies, learn to solve problems as a team! You can count on each other!

I can't stress enough the importance of time away from your role as mom. Every highly paid, highly stressful career known to man has built-in off-duty time. Make sure you create some for yourself.

This is part of what I want to help you understand about that dysfunctional belief you may have developed—that inner voice—that tries to say, "I'm not being a good mom if I don't include my kids in this," or "It's really selfish of me to want time to myself," or "My kids need me right now and they won't be young forever."

I say this without judging you. I have been there. I have thought those thoughts. I have believed those false beliefs.

I was at my wits' end by the time I first discovered Chick Night. Even though I had several friends attempt to explain this to me, I didn't understand what they were trying to say. Now that I look back on that time, it makes perfect sense to me that I just didn't get it. I was exhausted—mentally, physically, and emotionally exhausted. Big surprise that I couldn't hear what my friends were trying to tell me.

Trust me: you will be a *better* mom if you can learn to take time out for yourself. By spending time with other women, you will get a much-needed break from the 24/7 responsibility of motherhood. More important, you will reconnect with you, as a woman and as a person.

That feeling you have, that sensation that you are walking around in a perpetual state of "low battery," is exactly what has happened. You have given and given and given of yourself to the point of near depletion. Getting out for an evening that doesn't involve your children—not even as topics of conversation—will give you just the boost you've been hoping for.

In further explanation of this concept, I turn your attention to Section M, Subsection E of the Hanmer chapter of Chick Night regulations:

As a founding member of Chick Night it is your sworn duty to uphold the basic tenets of your chapter. During the course of any and all Chick Nights, you will solemnly promise to abdicate all duties and responsibilities associated with your multitasking roles of wife and mother. You will instead concentrate solely on nurturing *you*—the woman, the person, the individual.

Sounds simple enough, doesn't it?! Drop your roles and be yourself. Well, if you're anything like me, there is a very good chance that you are in for a bit of a shock. We'll talk about this in more detail with Rule #9: Keep It Real. For now, let me just forewarn you that stripping away your roles until you get down to you—just you—may not be as easy as you expect it to be. It all comes down to how long you have been giving them priority over the real you.

The process was a learning experience for all our founding members. Fortunately, practice makes perfect, and it was well worth it!

Step on It

by Collette Caza

You run out of the building. The getaway car is waiting at the curb with the motor running and the driver behind the wheel. You yell, "Step on it ... and don't look back!"

No, you haven't robbed a bank. You have just escaped for Chick Night.

As Bonnie's "white chocolate limo" backs out of my driveway, my children are waving from the window. They are both wearing a look of abandonment and rejection. My son and daughter are the respective ages of fifteen and eighteen.

Do I believe they can't live without Mom for one night a month? No. Am I having a hard time leaving them anyway? Yes! I tell myself it is because I take my mothering role seriously. However, there is more to it than that. I think the greatest problem in this area comes from the fact that children in our society are raised on breast milk and guilt. (Don't even try to pretend that you were not given this very same diet during many of your formative years.) As we reach adulthood, we develop the total belief that the only effective gas in our tanks of life is a good dose of guilt. That is why you can be quite sure that a mother's foot presses down firmly on that pedal.

As mothers, we feel like our families couldn't possibly get along without us. Then, when they do, we are somehow offended. The question is not "Can our children get along without us?" It is actually "Can we get along without our children?"

To figure out if you are going through what I did, ask yourself these two questions: Do I suddenly go into an identity crisis and have nothing to talk about unless my children are the conversation center? Do I somehow buy into the lie that my identity is only in my home and family?

If you answered yes (as I did six years ago), I dare you to take what I like to call the Collette Challenge. Start off slow and easy. Try, for one night a month, to be completely yourself!

The structure of Chick Night worked best for me, and you can try this too. You can allow Chick time to become the perfect opportunity to separate yourself from all your roles and titles. Separate the mom aspect of you and rediscover that there is a you aspect to you.

Come on. Try it. I dare you!

This was not a particularly easy rule for any of us to follow in the beginning. We had to learn to let go of the guilty feeling that we were somehow shirking our responsibilities by trying to have Chick time.

Collette's mother also has something to say on the topic of Chick Night:

Chick Night™ through a Mother's Eyes

by Eva Lanctot

As a mom of one of the Chicks, I want to say what is in my heart. Without the Chicks, I think my daughter would be very lonely, not having anyone to talk to about her problems and concerns. Would she have the same quality of life she now has if she didn't have the Chicks? I don't believe she would.

Of course, this is not to say that she couldn't talk to her mom about the molehills and mountains she has had to climb in her life. But perhaps for times when I was one of the molehills, what she really needed were the ears and hearts of her Chicks.

What I want to say to you, the readers of this book, is this: imagine knowing that every month, you too can have true friends to listen to your problems without judgment and with complete anonymity—friends who will always be there for you.

Imagine spending time with these most supportive and loving people, every month! WOW, how neat is that?

Whether your child is four months old or forty-plus years old, you never stop being a mom. That's why it is so important to take a break from this role when you can. Insisting that Chick Night be an *adults-only* club was a challenge at first, but over time it has become one of our most popular rules. We have learned to see ourselves apart from that role and to welcome the new perspective it provides.

Chick Night™ Rule #4:
Nothing Complicated

(Think KISS—Keep It Simple, Sister! Also known as the "No Migraines Allowed" Rule.)

Do you remember a time when no one could reach you once you left work or your house? No such luck now. In comparison to previous generations, our lives have gotten incredibly complicated. All the "time-saving" features of things, such as computers and cell phones and smartphones, have made it easier to get work done quickly; however, they have also made it easier for employers to get in touch, for work to be done at home, and for business hours to extend into evenings and weekends. It also means that no matter where you are or what you are doing, *everyone* can reach you 24/7!

Depending upon what technology you own, people can now phone you, text you, or even e-mail you wherever you are—with questions or with requests for additional work, errands, or rides. The worst part is that you are expected to respond immediately.

There is no such thing as running a few errands or grabbing a few groceries or enjoying a quiet cup of coffee or tea without interruption anymore. When I was growing up, the term *doctors' hours* was used to refer to someone who was on call 24/7. It seems like nearly everyone is in that boat these days!

Chick Night™ Rule #4A

Because of the nature of this nearly round-the-clock lifestyle, it is more important than ever for women to get a break from constant multitasking. It is for this reason that we, the founding members of Chick Night, decided to incorporate Rule #4.

The first thing we did was ban multitasking. In order to successfully accomplish this objective, we took our cue from movie theatres and created Section A, Subsection OK of the Hanmer chapter of Chick Night regulations, which should be read in a friendly, singsong voice:

> Attention, ladies. This evening's presentation of Chick Night is about to begin. Please turn off all cell phones and electronic devices to eliminate the possibility of distractions that might detract from your full enjoyment of this evening's festivities. Your cooperation in this matter is greatly appreciated. Thank you!

Depending on how hooked you are on technology, you may find our approach to this rule a tad extreme, but I can assure you that to fully appreciate all the pleasures and benefits of Chick Night, you need to follow our lead on this one. By making multitasking during Chick Night an "illegal act," we slyly gave ourselves a legitimate way to disconnect from all forms of communication other than talking to each other. It is a wonderful way to unplug from your responsibilities, even for just a few hours.

We took this extreme approach to make a point; however, we are realistic enough to know that sometimes *true* emergencies crop up and it is legitimately necessary for us to be reached immediately, instead of six hours from now. Our list of legitimate reasons for someone to track us down during Chick Night is actually quite short. It includes a house fire, a kidnapping, and the discovery that you have the four-million-dollar winning lottery ticket. In any of those cases, there is always someone at home who knows exactly where we are and has our express written permission to call us there.

Chick Night™ Rule #4B

The second part of Rule #4 borrows from the sentiment behind the adage "If it feels like work, it *is* work." Once you have confirmed the date for your next Chick Night, you will have successfully completed the most complicated part of the process. After that, keep it simple, sister!

Chick Night is one evening a month when you can just relax and have fun. No pressure. No worries. No stress. Therefore, if the evening you and the other founding members are trying to plan starts to seem as complicated as the seating arrangements for a royal wedding, just scrap those plans and do something simple instead. Here are some suggestions that we have tried, tested, and approved.

- Have dinner in a restaurant known for its great desserts. Let a professional buy the groceries, plan the menu, set your table, make your meal, serve your meal, clear off your table, and do your dishes. All you have to do is show up!
- Go shopping at your favourite bath-and-beauty-supply store, and then go for coffee or tea and dessert.
- Book a group manicure or pedicure appointment, and then go for coffee or tea and dessert.
- Have your makeup done by a professional and pose for a group photo. (Guess what I'm going to suggest you do afterward?)
- Switch into comfortable shoes and go for a long walk together—followed by a casual dessert at a local coffee shop.
- Visit a midway and ride on the Ferris wheel. (I definitely recommend the coffee/tea and dessert *after* this particular choice.)
- Go to an early movie and a late leisurely dinner—or vice versa.
- Rent a movie and curl up on a child-free sofa with enough popcorn for all.

Further to this suggestion, I recognize that renting movies can get tricky because at least one person in your group will already have seen every possible choice. That's why I am going to recommend selections from the following three categories:

- Classic Chick Flick (*Gone with the Wind, Dr. Zhivago,* or *Bridges of Madison County*)

- Inspirational Movie (*Fried Green Tomatoes, Beaches,* or *Steel Magnolias*)
- Fun Flick (*Miss Congeniality, Legally Blonde,* or *Mamma Mia!*)

The trick here is to pick a movie you have probably *all* seen but wouldn't mind seeing again. That way, if anyone in your group is the type who gets so excited about watching movies that she has a tendency to blurt out what is going to happen next (sorry, Bonnie and Collette—I'll *try* not to do that in the future), your overly exuberant but well-meaning (and dearly loved) friend won't spoil anyone's fun.

The simple, uncomplicated evenings tend to be the most fun. While I'm on the topic of simplicity, let me draw your attention once again to the Hanmer chapter of Chick Night regulations Section O, Subsection K:

> If the logistical coordination of a Chick Night should, at any time, begin to feel so complicated that it might give one or more members the slightest inclination toward a headache, said logistical co-ordination shall be terminated until such time as a low-maintenance solution can be found. Feeling stressed out about any aspect of Chick Night is strictly prohibited.

Sideswiped by Stress

Several years after the birth of Chick Night, we began having Chick Weekend once each summer. The first summer, Collette hosted it at her cottage, and the following summer Bonnie hosted it at her dad and stepmom's cottage. Because I don't have a cottage we can go to, our Chick Weekend for the third summer was going to be held at Collette's again. Fortunately, both of the Chicks recognized—and were willing to admit—that as hostess for the weekend, they had not enjoyed themselves as fully as they normally would. Each woman had felt a duty and a responsibility to look after her guests in a way that kept her slightly removed from the usual stress-free atmosphere of Chick time.

Without meaning to, we had broken our own rule. This would not do! The following year, we rented a cottage. We found that it was better to choose a location where we were all the guests. That way, after very simple planning, each of us could pitch in to share any chores (and all the fun) equally once we all arrived.

Stressful Stereotypes

One or more of your Chicks may have a background or an aptitude for event planning. If she actually enjoys the challenge of organizing monthly gatherings, you can call on her to work out all the details. Having said that, I urge you to make sure that each member of your chapter is able to look forward to upcoming Chick Nights as completely uncomplicated and stress-free evenings.

Chick Night is not a time for "the needs of the many to outweigh the needs of the few." Just because one member of your chapter is capable of organizing events doesn't necessarily mean she wants to. From time to time, it doesn't hurt to reassess who is responsible for what—and whether or not she actually wants to be. When that happens, be honest with yourself and each other.

Having fun is not supposed to feel like a chore. We already have more than enough of those! Besides, there is an element of logistics to nearly everything women do. We plan birthday parties, Halloween parties, Christmas parties, family celebration dinners, and summer vacations. We schedule work, classes, doctors' appointments, and errands. We organize and execute events ranging from children's sleepovers to out-of-town sports tournaments. All this happens on top of working and running a household.

Chick Night may be your only opportunity all month to have a completely fun and stress-free evening. It goes against everything Chick Night stands for if any members allow even the tiniest element of stress to creep into the process. Remember that the most important part of the evening is the women you are going to spend time with, laughing, sharing, and connecting. The where and what aren't nearly as essential as the who is. As long as you keep that in mind, the purpose of Rule #4 will be fulfilled and all of your Chick Nights will be special.

Chick Night™ Rule #5: Keep the Numbers Down

(More isn't always merrier.)

This rule deals with potentially sensitive situations. When word of your successful ventures into the realm of fun begins to spread, women will be literally popping up all around you. It won't take long before you begin to hear an enthusiastic chorus of "Can I join?" At the risk of seeming elitist, I strongly urge you and your founding members *not* to blurt out "Sure!" every time someone asks if she can come too.

There are two reasons for this. First of all, it will soon become apparent that trying to find one night every month when six or more women are all available will be next to impossible. An evening that requires a bus rental to get all the ladies to one location is probably not going to work very well either. Besides the fact that you will almost certainly find yourselves breaking Rule #2 (Once a Month) and Rule #4 (Nothing Complicated).

My second reason for this is a little more delicate. It involves the concept of balance. A nice, tight little group of three to five girlfriends, with a maximum of six, will quickly form a special bond. The more fun you share, the closer you will all become, and the more you will begin to count on each other as trusted confidantes. The addition of even *one* latecomer can tip the scale.

The Hanmer chapter of Chick Night official regulations document does not dwell on any unpleasantries. It simply addresses the question of new members in Section N, Subsection X:

No new members may be invited, either verbally or through

inference, without first being put to a vote. Only a unanimous verdict will result in invitation.

I sincerely hope that you will heed my warning; otherwise you could later find yourselves (as we eventually did) in the uncomfortable position of having to uninvite someone. This person will probably be a woman you all know and really like. There will be absolutely nothing "wrong" with her. However, the fact will remain that her presence somehow alters the balance of your group and the evenings will begin to seem awkward.

There is a gentle, unwritten, almost inexplicable balance that exists within every chapter of Chick Night. Tipping the scale can leave everyone feeling unhappy and unfulfilled. It is for this reason, even more than the first, that I strongly urge you to think carefully before adding additional members.

Now, before you vote to have me raked across the coals for "exclusionary practices," let me make my position clear. I am neither opposed nor suggesting that you be opposed to any woman—regardless of race, colour, creed, religious affiliation, political leaning, or personal viewpoint—as a potential member of your local Chick Night chapter. As far as I am concerned, as long as she is female, she is eligible. My only proviso here is the *number* of women you include in your group and *when* you choose to include them.

I have already given my reasons for this, but if you don't believe my points are valid, please read the following letter from my friend Heather. I asked her to write down her thoughts after we had a conversation about an experience she and her girlfriends had a few years ago:

> My group consists of six members. We have built a solid relationship foundation over the past fifteen years and thoroughly enjoy one another's company. Recently, a friend outside the group showed an interest in joining our group. Collectively, we decided to add this new member.
>
> After a few months, however, we noticed that the entire dynamic of the group had changed and wasn't working any more.
>
> The original members decided that it was important, for the good of the group, to change things back to the way they were. I'm

happy to report that our original crew is back to normal and loving spending time together!

I've given this a lot of thought since then and have come to the conclusion that if someone brings negativity and pain into your life, you have the right to end that relationship. As women, we often feel guilty when it comes to situations like this. However, we should not allow anyone to bring us down.

Dealing with guilt can feel like you've been asked to slay a dragon with a butter knife, but it really is well worth the effort. Life presents us with enough challenges already. Better to convert those "challenges" into opportunities for personal growth. (See Rule #8 for more in-depth discussion on this topic.)

Mentoring Versus More Members

Instead of feeling compelled to include every woman who voices her desire to come, encourage each of them to start her own chapter. Can you imagine what a happy country this would be if we had ten thousand chapters of Chick Night? The next time a woman asks about Chick Night or starts dropping hints that she would like to be invited, offer to mentor her as she opens her own chapter. Make her a copy of the Ten to Remember. Or, better yet, give her a copy of this book.

Share your chapter's successes and experiences with her as you guide her through the process of creating friendships that will carry her through a lifetime of her own successes and experiences. Encourage her to begin now. There is no "right age" to get started. No matter what stage of life she is now living, no matter what her life circumstances happen to be, today is the day to make that first call, to that first woman, to make that first suggestion for their first Chick Night.

To illustrate my point, I would like to introduce you to three women who are each from a different generation of the same family. My friend Rhonda has just barely reached her fifties; her mom, Donna, has just barely waved good-bye to her sixties; and Rhonda's daughter, Raili, is just beginning her twenties. Each of these women has her own perspective on Chick Night. They have graciously agreed to share them, starting with Rhonda.

My Ya-Yas

by Rhonda Lakanen

I've always been an enthusiastic member of some female bonding group ... from the after-school clubs in elementary school to the group of BFFs* (before BFF was even an expression!) in high school, and from my two closest friends in university (the three of us are all in different cities but still get together every few years) to my current group of close friends, the Ya-Yas.

The Ya-Yas (named from the novel *The Divine Secrets of the Ya-Ya Sisterhood*) got together as a group in the late 1990s. There are seven of us, all having met through various connections in our small town. We soon discovered that, aside from having children close in age and frequenting the same places (dance studios, hockey rinks, school fun fairs), we shared a love of laughter and a willingness to connect. Although we are similar in many ways, we are also very different in our outlooks, career choices, and the way we handle conflict, but we've grown to appreciate those differences, and that keeps it interesting!

Since starting to hang out together, we have had many fun times, from our walking club to milestone birthdays (yep, we all made it through the big 4-0 and are now experiencing hitting the next "big" one!) to awesome Ya-Ya trips (our New York adventure was a cross of *Sex and the City* and *The Golden Girls*) to our regular Ya-Ya birthday dinners (that means seven dinners out at various restaurants every year) to our impromptu get-togethers at one of our homes or cottages.

Through all of this, we have laughed ourselves silly over inside jokes and cried together when one of us is going through a particularly challenging time. Always, we know we can count on one another to ferry children, provide muffins or a hot meal, make sure we have enough chocolate during stressful conversations, and mostly to have each other's backs. My life is richer because of these female friendships and I am happy to celebrate the "Ya-Yas" in all our lives!

*For the record, BFF stands for "Best Friends Forever."

Now let's hear from Rhonda's mom, Donna:

The Evolution of Friendships

by Donna Burden

I was sipping my tea today and reminiscing about mornings I enjoyed with a group of friends when we were all in our early thirties. I chuckled to myself as I pictured us all around my best friend's table, puffing on cigarettes in a cloud of smoke and blissfully unaware of what we were doing to our health. We covered a lot of ground every morning. We would discuss our kids, husbands, old boyfriends, "what-ifs," recipes, decorating, and, of course, the big "sex" always worked its way into the conversation.

Now, forty years later, I meet with another group of ladies whose ages range from sixty to ninety ... and the conversation has changed drastically. The topics now are mostly health-related, such as cataracts, colonoscopies, incontinence, and hip replacements. We also talk about funerals and the weather (how come it seems so much colder now than when we were younger?), but one topic that is never mentioned is the *S* word.

I was comparing the two different age groups and found that my preference would have to be for the older group. I don't know if it is because, as you mature, you don't feel that you are in competition with anyone or that, in your ripe old age, you gain confidence and reassurance.

It's amusing to watch the older ladies ask to have half their lunch wrapped to go (with the expectation of not having to cook supper) and then forget the package on the table. This is a very common occurrence! It's also fun to observe us peering over our glasses when we take a break from studying the menu to speak to the others at the table. These are silly little things that would probably go unnoticed by others, but to me, they are very endearing.

During the winter months, a few of the ladies travel south, and upon their return, they receive a genuine, warm welcome from everyone with a big hug and smile. I look forward to seeing "the girls" every second Tuesday of the month … and does that month ever go by quickly!

The gist of this story is that if you have one friend or many friends—be they young or old—you are very blessed and your world is a better place because of them.

We've heard from Mom and Grandma. Now let's hear from Raili.

Growing Up While Growing Closer

by Raili Lakanen

This Christmas, as with every holiday season, three of my girlfriends from high school and I met up to exchange gifts, gab about school, and eat lots of good food. It's been years since we graduated, and we're all at different universities pursuing graduate or second degrees, but we're still bonded by our similar interests, shared experiences, and genuine care for one another.

Though I have many crowds of female friends, I've stayed particularly close with my "girls"—our group of four from high school. We connected over our shared love of performing and spent a great deal of time together staying late at school for musical theatre rehearsals and shows. It was also in high school that we solidified our most treasured ritual: girls' night. Girls' night consists of an old-fashioned slumber party, complete with Chick flicks, Chick chat, and our favourite snack foods (and now that we're older, some wine!).

Girls' nights are such an important tradition because they give us quality time to spill all our news and know that we will get a sympathetic ear, a sense of humour, and the best advice. Something I really value about my girls is that they are all real people, with complex personalities that cannot be distilled into one stereotype or archetypal character; in fact, one ill-fated attempt to identify who would be each character from *Sex and the City* gave us many laughs and some good-hearted disagreements, and ultimately taught us that we love and appreciate one another for our complications and intricacies.

I appreciate that my girls will tell me like it is. They are the ones who will honestly give their opinion on the dress you're trying on or the haircut you're considering, and are really, truly brave enough to offer the toughest phrase in Chick advice: "Maybe he's just not that into you." We've seen each other through the drama and angst of high school, the loneliness and lonesomeness when we first moved away from home, and some of the toughest breakups and other losses we've ever known.

Now that we're older and have lived in different cities over the years, we still make attempts to visit one another and keep in touch when we can. We've found that, because it's getting harder to keep up with the day-to-day of one another's lives when we're so busy with our own experiences, girls' nights are even more important. When we're munching on Smartfood popcorn and marshmallow strawberries, sharing our new goals and congratulating one another on our achievements, spilling details about our latest adventures, and giggling like teenagers, it's easy to see why our cherished ritual—and our friendship—is so valuable to me.

These three wonderful women can attest to the fact that true friendship lasts—regardless of age, regardless of generation, and regardless of life circumstances. Thanks for sharing, ladies!

Chick Night™ Rule #6: Don't Let Money Be an Issue

(Lack of funds does not mean lack of fun.)

This is one of my favourite rules (besides #1, of course) because it encourages women to exercise their imaginations. Anyone can whip out a credit card and yell, "Time to party!" This rule requires the use of creativity, and it eliminates an obstacle we have all considered very real at one time or another.

One of our best Chick Nights was the result of a last-minute change in plans, and it cost absolutely nothing. One of the Chicks thought she wouldn't be able to get away for the night, so we showed up at her house an hour after Chick Night was supposed to start, armed with desserts we had thrown together from ingredients already in our fridges, freezers, and cupboards.

Imagine her surprise when we barged into her kitchen with a suitably large serving dish of Chocolatey Goodness (see end of chapter for recipe).

Those beer ads don't know what they're talking about. *Nothing* starts a party faster than a gooey chocolate dessert! Within minutes, we were all howling with laughter. The evening went on for three pots of tea, generous seconds of ... (well, I don't mean Brussels sprouts), and enough jokes and funny stories to lift everyone's spirits sky-high.

In the end, the evening was deemed "a hoot" (the highest possible compliment) by all present. Much later in the evening, we slightly bent, without actually breaking, Rule #3 when we allowed her teenage children to come out for a slice of dessert. We figured, since we wrote the list, that we could bend or temporarily revise it if we wanted to. (Our only stipulation with any temporary revisions or permanent rewrites of the rules of Chick Night is that the decision has to be unanimous.)

I have told you about this one particular Chick Night in our chapter history to illustrate a point. It is not necessary to spend oodles of money to have a good time.

Starting a List

We have done everything from decorating Easter eggs to having a themed sleepover. Believe me, there is nothing more hysterical than a living room full of pillows, sleeping bags, and full-grown women in Winnie-the-Pooh pyjamas.

Chick Night does not have to be an expensive proposition. There are plenty of things you can do together that involve little or no money. This is a short list Bonnie, Collette, and I came up with:

- Rent a movie.
- Go window-shopping at your favourite mall.
- Walk along a boardwalk or through a local art gallery or museum.
- Take a stroll through the park and push each other on the swings.
- Pack a picnic lunch and go for a hike or to an open-air concert in the park.
- Grab your cameras before you head outdoors. Take interesting pictures of your surroundings and fun photos of each other, and then share them later by print, slide show, or e-mail.
- Make ice cream (with an ice cream maker) or other yummy desserts and meet for a "sweet smorgasbord" at one of your girlfriends' kitchen tables.
- Draw upon the skills and resources of your Chicks for anything and everything from crafts or scrapbooking to tennis or kayaking.
- Play cards or a favourite board game from your childhood.
- Combine talents, energy, and creativity to help each other plant your gardens or take care of a chore that won't seem like a chore when it's shared.

- Look for opportunities to provide random acts of kindness, sharing your good fortune with others.

The issue of money was handled quite cleverly (we think) in the Hanmer chapter of Chick Night regulations Section Cha, Subsection Ching:

> After careful consideration of all viewpoints, concerns, perceptions, facts, and fiction, it has been decided that lack of funds is not deemed relevant to the execution of Chick Night.

As they say in the theatre, the show must go on! So too must Chick Night.

On a personal note, let me just say that I have absolutely nothing against spending money. Sometimes, the activity or event you agree to go to will cost you some cash. There is nothing wrong with a well-spent dollar (or two, or ten). The only thing Rule #6 is designed for is to get you thinking so that you don't allow lack of funds to keep you from having fun.

This is what Laurie (my BFF since high school) e-mailed when I asked for her suggestions on inexpensive things to do on Chick Night:

> In our group of women, we range in age from early forties to late fifties and have a wide variety of disposable-income ranges. This has never been an issue for us because our get-togethers are inexpensive, for the most part. When we get together, even though some of these women live far outside of the city limits, we have a close bond and connection that has nothing to do with where or how we live or how much we earn.
>
> The important thing when planning something like this is to make sure the company you're with is fun and that everyone intends to make each other feel good about themselves. I know some of my most fun times have had nothing to do with money. I had fun because of whom I was with!
>
> Here's something I've done that has been and continues to be a lot of fun. A group of us meet at a girlfriend's house for an evening of amateur tarot card readings. It's a great way to relax

and enjoy yourself. You can bring your own cards or get on the Web and go to a free site. You get to pick one question about yourself and the others get to pick one question for you. This, along with a couple of bottles of wine and pleasant company, makes for a lot of laughs.

If tarot card readings aren't your cup of tea, how about four girlfriends getting together and inviting four really good-looking guys over to play Twister? I have not yet done this, but it sounds interesting, doesn't it? Remember to invite me and my group of friends if this is your choice of activity. We will bring the wine.

I do love Laurie's sense of humour (or perhaps that was an example of her sense of adventure). Another friend, Katherine, e-mailed her suggestions:

When I was younger and poorer, my girlfriends and I would sit on a bench on Main Street with an ice cream cone and watch the guys drive around and around the "circuit." It was a very small town with a main drag about a mile long. Once, my friend Laura and I figured we'd have one over on the guys, so we made "lap cards." The cards started at lap 3. Whenever the guys would come around for the fourth and fifth times, we'd be there holding our cards up. Usually it took until lap 7 for them to figure out what we were doing. It was fun!

We also used to all pile into a car and go for a "boo-rah" (an aimless drive) through the forest roads.

When all else failed, we'd head to the harbour and watch the sailboats or sit by the river. Sometimes we'd even have a fire going in a pit. We also used to go horseback riding or canoeing.

Now, as an adult, I have a girlfriend who will go with me to an old graveyard. We walk around reading the headstones and just talking.

This is all a matter of priority. Young children don't have bank or credit cards, cheques, or wallets, but they never have trouble coming up with ways to have fun.

If this is a skill you and your girlfriends have lost, it's time to relearn it. Once you do, lack of money or available cash will never slow you down again. The sad phrase "I'd love to, but I can't afford it" will completely lose its power over you. That, my friend, is a *wonderful* freedom.

I have total faith in you. Regardless of how you and your Chicks decide to spend your evening, I would like to take this moment to applaud your affirmative action plan. North American culture has placed far too much importance (and therefore, stress) on spending money. In fact, it is well known that money is one of the top three stressors in our society. Fortunately for you, Chick Night has built-in stress-relief measures, including our Rule #6. This reminds me: in case your chapter has decided to have a chocolate fondue night, you need to be aware of Section C (for Chocolate), Subsection 3B:

> Speaking with one's mouth full is permissible under the following conditions:
>
> - The Chick's mouth is full of chocolate (which we all know deserves to be savoured and enjoyed).
> - The Chick is using positive reinforcement in response to another Chick's comment.
> - The Chick has just remembered a particularly motivating, funny, or empowering anecdote.
> - The Chick is expressing appreciation for the love, support, and friendship of her fellow Chicks.
> - The Chick's mouth is full of chocolate (this one is worth repeating).

Before I forget, it would be cruel to specifically mention a dessert and not give you the recipe. Here it is:

Chocolatey Goodness

Syrup:
1½ cups brown sugar
1½ cups water

2 Tbs. butter

Bring to a boil. Remove from heat.

Batter:

2 Tbs. margarine

1 tsp. vanilla

½ cup sugar

1 cup flour

2 tsp. baking powder

4 Tbs. cocoa

¾ cup milk

¼ cup chopped walnuts (optional)

Mix well. Pour into greased 8-inch cake pan. Pour syrup over batter. Bake at 350 degrees for 30 minutes (or until batter is cake consistency).

Chick Night™ Rule #7: The Confidentiality Clause

(It's okay to spill tea, but never spill secrets.)

Depending upon what you are looking for, you may choose to form a Chick Night chapter that consists of female extended-family members who enjoy spending time together or female coworkers who appreciate the opportunity to let off a little steam with women who fully understand their stresses. Many founding members of Chick Night chapters will start out as casual acquaintances (coworkers, neighbours, women you've met at your child's day care, school, or sports activities, and so on).

Whatever level of friendship you want to develop from that point on will be entirely up to you and is perfectly acceptable. Your Chick Night chapter will become what you collectively make of it.

If you decide to invest the time and trust required, you most definitely have the option of developing close, deep relationships with women who could ultimately prove to be lifelong friends and confidantes.

One of the greatest gifts you can accept from Chick Night is the evolution of relationships with the other women in your group— relationships that will ultimately bring you great joy and a deeper level of understanding and compassion for each other and for yourself. After enough Chick Nights, the relationship you have with these women has the capacity to grow deeper and much more meaningful if, and only if, there is total trust between all of you.

There's a very good reason why many companies insist that their employees and executives sign confidentiality agreements when they are hired. These agreements protect businesses from costly information leaks to their competitors. When it comes to Chick Night, confidentiality is even more important because it is not just about money. It's about trust.

The Hanmer chapter of Chick Night regulations Section Q, Subsection T leaves no room for loopholes in this matter:

> Each member of Chick Night has the right, and will exercise the right, to complete and total confidentiality. Nothing that is said, inferred, or alluded to over the course of any given Chick Night will be repeated, or even hinted at, without the express written permission of each and every member of said Chick Night chapter. End of discussion.

Think of the incredible value confidentiality will add to your quality of life. Being able to actually say what you are thinking is an extremely liberating experience. Outside of Chick Night, how often can you speak freely? When and where can you express your opinions or concerns, your hopes and dreams without fear of their being repeated, judged, or mocked afterward? At Chick Night, there are no bosses or supervisors, no husbands or children, no mothers or in-laws or nosy neighbours listening to your every word. This may be your only chance for conversations that can be so open. You can speak from your heart, completely uncensored.

If the practice of honouring confidentiality has been a problem for you in the past, now is your opportunity to break that pattern forever. If you consistently open your heart and close your mouth, the rest will take care of itself.

I cannot stress strongly enough how very, very important this is! Without a personal guarantee of confidentiality among Chick Night members, there can be no trust. Without trust, there can be no bond, and without a bond, there is no Chick Night!

Understand from the start that a breach of trust cannot be mended. It doesn't matter how interesting, surprising, shocking, or juicy your conversation gets: what was said during Chick Night *stays* with Chick Night. *No blabbing.* Nothing, I repeat, nothing allows any member of Chick Night to break this solemn pact of confidentiality.

Learning to trust and being trusted is a reward beyond measure. It is a direct pathway to connecting with yourself and others. Being on the giving and the receiving end of this level of trust is priceless. Put away your chequebooks, ladies. This is one of those intangible life lessons that is worth its weight in gold. Many have sought it, but none have bought it. Feel free to accept this bonus feature of Chick Night with my compliments.

S.O.S. (Save Our Sister) Chick Night™

The term S.O.S. is popularly (although incorrectly) believed to stand for several messages, including "Save Our Souls," and "Save Our Ship." Although the letters themselves actually have no meaning, S.O.S. dates back to the days of Morse code and is a universally recognizable distress call. Mariners knew that hearing this call for help meant, "Drop everything and get here fast. Your immediate assistance is required."

The founding members of the Hanmer chapter of Chick Night chose to put our own special spin on S.O.S. For us, it stands for "Save Our Sister."

There is one additional twist to the S.O.S. Chick Night. The woman in distress is *not* the one who uses the signal. In fact, quite often the woman who really needs it is not even aware that her situation constitutes an emotional emergency. Such is the sad truth. Many women have spent so little of their time and energy keeping in touch with their feelings that they may not fully recognize the level of their own distress.

That is why the founders of the Hanmer chapter of Chick Night decided that responsibility for calling an S.O.S. Chick Night would fall to others. When two or more Chick Night members notice that one of their own is dealing with a personal crisis, it is up to *them* to sound the alarm. In a way, it's like being the last one invited to the party. The decision to save our sister is made by members of the group who sense that their sister needs the love, support, and chocolate that can be found only in a Chick Night setting.

The very first S.O.S. Chick Night we ever had was called by Bonnie and Collette on my behalf. I was in the midst of a parenting crisis that felt like it was rocking the very foundations of my world. It seems a melodramatic statement to make (even to me) now that the situation has been resolved, but at the time it was extremely unnerving.

As Collette and Bonnie well know, I have a rather annoying habit of trying to deal with most things on my own. I usually end up telling the two of them about the situation when it's all over. I'm not purposely trying to keep them out of the loop. I just seem to react that way.

In this particular instance, they both felt a sense of alarm after reading an e-mail note from me. Within one day of sending my chatty (or so I thought) note, I received a summons to an S.O.S Chick Night. I was given the date, time, and location, and told to "come unarmed." (That's Chick-speak for "We'll provide the chocolate. You just bring *you*.")

I can't even begin to describe the wonderful all-encompassing sense of love, security, and emotional support I received that evening. I talked, I cried, and I confessed my fears, and then we all worked out a plan of action. Within two days, my perceived "crisis" had been properly dealt with and resolved. It all seems so straightforward now (mainly because the use of hindsight is the ultimate form of cheating), but at the time it felt insurmountable.

Nobody ever said parenting was easy. Since all three of us are moms, we have each had our share of "moments." Several years ago, I gave Collette a quick call about something (I don't even remember what it was) and sensed that something was wrong the second she answered the phone. She was so distraught, she simply told me what had happened and then ended the call. Within half an hour, Bonnie and I were on her doorstep with a tub of chocolate ice cream, three spoons, and a box of tissues.

The rest of the evening was spent simply listening. We gave no advice. We expressed no opinions. What we gave instead was our support and compassion. Sometimes, that is all your Chick will want or need. It will be important for you, as a group, to be able to recognize the difference between these two scenarios—and what your Chick really needs from you.

These examples represent one of the ways an S.O.S. Chick Night can be called. Over the years, more than one of us has also requested it for herself, and in one particular case, it came about at the request of a hubby.

Allow me to introduce Dan Paquette, Bonnie's husband …

S.O.S. Chick Night™ through a Husband's Eyes

by Dan Paquette

As a husband of one of the Chicks, I have greatly appreciated the fact that the Chicks have developed such a good friendship and bond over the years. It is important for them to meet on a regular basis because they spend time together uplifting and encouraging one another.

I also enjoy seeing the Chicks have fun together, especially when they are having their loads of laughter. It is a good way for them to get rid of stress.

There was a time, not that many years ago, when Bonnie was particularly struggling with the pressure of being overworked. I had heard her mention that they had something called S.O.S. Chick Nights, so I called one of the Chicks to alert her to how Bonnie was feeling. Within an hour of my phone call, both Chicks were here at the house, offering Bonnie their unconditional support.

I feel blessed that they are there for my wife in times of need. I know that these women are friends who are there for her no matter what.

Speaking as a husband, I think every woman would benefit from having such good friends in her life.

As a bit of a background to this story, I think it important to mention that when Dan first came on the scene, Bonnie and Collette and I had already been doing Chick Night for several years. As a newlywed, Dan was slightly put off by the fact that we kept swiping his wife one Saturday night per month, which meant one less potential date night with his new bride.

Dan happened to casually mention this to Collette's husband, whose name is also Dan. (Can you imagine how confusing this gets sometimes?) Collette's Dan looked Bonnie's Dan straight in the eye and said, "The Chicks were here before you were."

That was many years ago, and it is obvious that Bonnie's Dan now agrees with Collette's Dan in recognizing the importance of the bond between the Chicks. As her friends, Collette and I were more than willing to honour that bond by responding promptly to the S.O.S. Chick Night that Bonnie's husband, Dan, initiated.

When the time comes for you and your girlfriends to form a Chick Night chapter of your own, I strongly recommend that you make S.O.S. Chick Night a part of your group's sacred mandate. There is no greater gift you can give each other than your love and compassion. Believe me, it will be accepted and cherished.

On a practical level, an S.O.S. Chick Night offers the woman in crisis the very real benefit of the calm and insightful viewpoint of women who are in a position to see the whole picture. My mom has often voiced the old saying, "You can't always see the forest for the trees." This particularly wise statement is especially applicable in highly emotional situations. When two or more Chick Night members offer to listen to their fellow Chick's crisis, they are able to step back and view all the issues from a completely different vantage point. This allows them to offer less emotionally charged thoughts and reactions.

One thing the woman in distress must be aware of is that there is no guarantee she will *like* everything she hears. There may be something she *needs* to hear but does not particularly *want* to hear. The one consolation I can offer (from personal experience) is that the pill isn't quite so bitter when delivered by a friend who is being lovingly honest. You will not have to worry about these sentiments being expressed out of anger, sarcasm, jealousy, or pettiness. Your Chicks have your best interests at heart. S.O.S. Chick Night was created to provide a safe environment for a woman to face her fears, stare directly at her issues, and summon the courage to take positive steps toward dealing with them.

The camaraderie and support of Chick Night is more valuable (in terms of your quality of life) than any dollar figure you or I could ever arbitrarily assign. I urge you to establish and nurture relationships with girlfriends. The rewards they bring you will last a lifetime.

Chick Night™ Rule #8: Never Do Guilt about Chick Night™

(It's one night a month and you deserve it!)

Autopilot Guilt

The habit of automatically feeling guilty—even if it's not your fault or responsibility—can be extremely debilitating. I'm talking about that one-size-fits-all type of guilt that automatically kicks in when you want to do something for yourself.

It is triggered approximately 0.00000001 seconds after you casually entertain the thought of having an evening out with friends. When you are in the throes of autopilot guilt, your mind immediately begins to list all the "reasons" why you shouldn't. Most of these so-called reasons include words like *might* or *could* or *probably* ... as in "This might inconvenience ..." or "This could be a problem for ..." or "This will probably interfere with ...," and so on. In other words, you don't even know if it will be an issue for anyone, but you're already talking yourself out of the plans you have yet to make.

Why do women do this? It is as if someone programmed us to default to the "guilt" setting. I will talk about "mother guilt" in a minute, but this has nothing to do with whether or not you have children. I know teenagers who do this and I know single, highly successful career women in their forties who do this: apologize for everything. They feel guilty without questioning whether they did anything to feel guilty about. Worse still, they deny themselves all kinds of enjoyment and relaxation because they choose to assume there is something wrong or selfish or undisciplined about wanting a little fun. I am hoping that, by bringing this up, I can encourage you to look inside yourself to see if you are doing it.

Experts will tell you that it takes thirty days to learn a new habit. This is my challenge to you: every time you feel guilty about what you hope to do for yourself for the next thirty days, go and talk to the person you think will be upset or inconvenienced by those plans. There is a very good chance that the person will wonder why you even thought he or she would mind. If the person has a legitimate objection to your plans, try to work out some sort of compromise that will allow both of you to feel good about the decision.

Try this for thirty days. That's all I ask. At the end of the thirty days, take stock of how often your autopilot is kicking in as opposed to how often you are beginning to actually do the things you'd like to do.

I know you can do this. I believe in you.

Mother Guilt

No one has ever been able to prove it, but every woman knows that at some point during the labour and delivery of her first child, the doctor injects her with a lifetime dosage of "mother guilt."

It must be true. It's the only plausible explanation for why perfectly sane, rational, levelheaded women allow themselves to be totally and completely wrapped around the little, and I mean little, fingers of their children. Even the most stoic and determined of women can be reduced to a quivering mass of self-doubting, indecisive jelly at the slightest indication of a tiny pair of teary eyes. God forbid it be a whimper or the plaintive, barely audible whisper of the word *mommy*. The most independent and self-sufficient of women have been known to completely fall apart—resolve broken and determination shattered.

How many times have you cancelled plans for an evening out because you felt guilty about leaving your child? How long has it been since you even bothered to make plans to go out, for the same reason?

Take heart, ladies! I have the mother guilt antidote you have been hoping for—and I'm giving it away for free! It's 100 percent natural, totally effective, has no hidden side effects, and lasts a lifetime once administered. The antidote you have been seeking is ... a dose of reality.

There's no sense mixing this medicine with honey, because chances are, you're not going to like the taste of it on first swallow. The reality is ... your child *will* survive the "trauma" of you going out. Those precious few hours you devote to yourself will *not* emotionally scar your child for life. In fact, chances are pretty good that, ten minutes after you leave the house, your little one will be fully engaged in the carefree play that comes naturally to kids.

Trust me when I tell you, mother to mother, that everything will be okay. Honest! I cannot guarantee that the good-bye scene at the door won't tear at your heartstrings, but I do promise you that both mother and child *will* survive it.

More reality: mother and child won't just survive ... You will both flourish! If you are a stay-at-home mom, you have spent *every moment of every day*, for months (maybe even years) with your child. If you are a working mom, you have spent every evening, weekend, and statutory holiday for months (maybe even years) with your child. You have fed, changed, burped, bathed, cuddled, and played with your children during times that the rest of the world carried on without you. At first, this was your choice. There was nowhere else you wanted to be more than with your baby. After a while, it simply became *the only place you were.*

It is amazing to me how very quietly and unconsciously this happens. Mothers can get themselves into a rut by doing exactly what they've always dreamed of doing: being a mother. (I sure wish they would talk about *this* in those prenatal classes!) The longer a woman goes without a break from her child, the harder it becomes to even contemplate the idea. She worries that her child won't be able to handle the stress of separation, even for a few hours, but the *real* issue is that Mommy isn't sure if *she* can handle it. "What if my baby cries or fusses while I'm gone?!" Your little one may do one or both of those things, but in the big picture you will actually be doing your child a *favour* by going out for a while.

The best way I can explain what I mean by that last statement is to ask you to think of yourself as the Energizer Bunny. You have been going and going and going for a very long time, willingly giving of your time, energy, and love to your family with no signs of slowing down or stopping. Without realizing it, you have been draining your battery. After all this time, there's not much juice left. If you don't recharge your battery soon, you won't have anything left to give. That's reality.

Make sure you will be able to *continue* doing what you're doing by reenergizing yourself in the company of women you love, trust, and have fun with. That's part of what Chick Night is for: to provide women with the opportunity to recharge their batteries.

Take a page out of the Hanmer chapter of Chick Night regulations Section G, Subsection O:

> All women in attendance at an officially sanctioned Chick Night will be present in not only body, but mind and spirit as well. Said women will concentrate on themselves and their enjoyment, focussing on guilt-free pleasure. Henceforth and hereafter, all members of Chick Night will engage in such frivolity and merriment as is unanimously agreed upon, fully understanding the future rewards and benefits to all family members.

Self-Worth

I know, I know, everybody talks about self-esteem and self-worth. Those two terms have been so overused in the past couple of decades that discussions on the importance of having high self-esteem and a strong sense of self-worth are bordering on cliché. It may seem like the words themselves have little or no effect, but the concepts are just as relevant and important as they were when the whole self-help movement first began.

Of all the important things you will (ideally) figure out in your lifetime, recognizing your own self-worth is definitely in the top three. Until you truly understand your own importance—your own value—you will be hopelessly stuck in a cycle of self-loathing and guilt. Nothing you ever do will seem good enough. Nothing you ever say will seem smart enough. Nothing you ever think will seem wise enough. No matter how little you weigh or how you wear your hair or how you apply your makeup or how much you spend on your clothes and jewellery, you will never feel pretty enough.

Do you know why that is? It's because your perception of yourself is "I'm *not good enough.*"

You can do every exterior type of makeover known to civilization, but until you reach deep inside yourself and discover that you really, truly, honestly, for real *are* good enough, you will never recognize or accept that you are.

Personal self-worth is one of the hardest concepts I have ever had to grasp. I put myself through a lot of crap, accepted a lot of crummy treatment, and begged people I was better off without to stay in my life because I didn't think I deserved better. In fact, at the time, I didn't even think I deserved that much.

I'm amazed when I look back on some of the things that I put up with, the things that life had to dish out for me to *finally* say, "Oh, I don't think so! Enough is enough! I deserve better than this! I *am* better than this!"

Out of life's biggest challenges come the greatest gifts. It took me a while to realize that, but I sure understand it now. Not only do I understand it, but I am truly grateful for it. I am really and truly grateful for what I've gone through because it ripped off the rose-coloured glasses and forced me to take an honest look at the treatment I was receiving and the fact that *I had asked for it*!

Yes, ladies. That free dose of reality I offered you as an antidote for mother guilt is also a wonder cure when applied to the other issues in your life. Reality was a hard pill for me to swallow at first, but it was absolutely true. Everything that was happening in my life right then was happening because on some level I believed it was what I deserved. It's what I believed, so it's exactly what I got.

It was rather a huge "ouch" when I finally figured this out.

Once the initial sting of realization wore off, I began to understand that because I was the one in control of what I was getting—based on what I believed I deserved—it stood to reason that I was also the one who could *change* what I was getting, by *changing* what I believed I deserved.

This realization is liberating. It allows you to put yourself back in the driver's seat of your own life. Instead of believing who you are and what you deserve based on the way other people treat you, you can *choose* to believe better about yourself.

This process will take some time. It will require you to look at how you see yourself and decide if your previous self-assessment has been accurate or unfair. That's where your Chick Night friends can help. They will be there to love and support you through your journey (and you will be able to do the same thing for them). They will also be there to point out your good qualities and your strengths, in case you can't clearly see them yet (and again, you will be able to do the same thing for them).

So here we are back at self-worth. How much *are* you worth? This question does not refer to your net worth in terms of taxable income or investments or the value of your property. Self-worth is about you as a person. It is about how you feel about yourself deep down in your very core. This is the information that you have probably kept hidden from others and may even have kept hidden from yourself until now.

I repeat my question: how much are you worth? It is crucial that you ask yourself this fundamental question because what you believe you are worth is directly related to how much you think you deserve. It reflects your inner viewpoint on how you deserve to be spoken to, how you deserve to be treated, and whether or not you are on your own list of the important people in your life. Let's put it this way: if you don't think you deserve one night a month out with the girls, one guilt-free night of fun to enjoy yourself in the company of women who love and respect you, then it's probably time for you to go inward and look at your self-worth.

You may want to take a chocolate break here for a few minutes. Get your bearings and then continue to read, as we look at another element of guilt that may be tripping you up in your efforts to embark on a successful series of Chick Nights.

Kick Those Guilty Feelings to the Curb and Get Behind the Wheel of Your Own Life!

Self-Care

This topic is an aspect of self-worth that for many women, me included, needs to be tackled on an ongoing basis because its importance can easily be forgotten.

Self-care covers more than the standard trio of getting enough sleep, eating healthful food, and staying physically active. Although these three practices are important, they don't paint the full picture. There is another element of self-care that, if ignored, can cause women to fall headfirst into the guilt trap. I am referring to that internal voice of condemnation that begins to holler at you the moment you forget to be gentle with yourself.

Being gentle with yourself includes:

- Accepting the fact that there are only so many hours in a day and there is only so much you can accomplish during those hours. Chastising yourself with all the things you "could" and "should" have done today is a colossal waste of your time and energy. Ease off on the pressure by avoiding unrealistic expectations and focussing on the positive results of your day.
- Eliminating the negative effect of self-recrimination when you think you've made a mistake or taken a misstep. Being gentle with yourself is a conscious choice. Wouldn't you rather be one of your strongest supporters than one of your harshest critics?
- Allowing yourself the right to make decisions based on what is best for you. It's fine and dandy to think of others first, but that doesn't mean you shouldn't think about yourself at all! Before ruling out a decision based on your assumption about how it will affect others, take a look at how *not* making that decision will affect you.

It is this final point that I want to address in the greatest detail. I will use an example that is applicable to Chick Night: there will come a time when you need to cancel out on one of your Chick Night get-togethers. There are many *legitimate* reasons why you might have to take a rain check. These include, but are not limited to, a family emergency, out-of-town relatives dropping in unexpectedly, kids getting sick, or you getting sick. In other words, instances when *life happens*.

This can pose a challenge. How does a woman committed to Chick Night and loyal to her Chick Night friends cancel those plans without feeling guilty about it? This is the moment that self-care meets self-worth, and you will need to remind yourself that honouring yourself and your needs is not selfish or thoughtless or inconsiderate or rude or wrong. Respecting yourself enough to recognize that you have the *right* to back out of a Chick Night if you want or need to is *a good thing*.

Each member of the Hanmer chapter of Chick Night has been faced with this challenge at one time or another. All three of us found it tough to deal with this because our initial reaction was to feel guilty. We didn't want to disappoint the other two. All three of us felt guilty, even though we *knew* the others would completely understand our reason for having to cancel.

There were never any hard feelings.

This instant reaction of guilt was just emotional garbage we piled on our own shoulders.

Why do we do this to ourselves? Why do we automatically assume that the happiness of others is more important than our own happiness? It took Bonnie, Collette, and me some time to realize that those guilty feelings pointed to our individual attitudes toward self-worth. Each of us knew that the other two were true friends and that neither of them would be disappointed, hurt, or angry by our need to reschedule a Chick Night. In fact, in all three cases, we insisted that there was no point in even having a Chick Night if one of us was not going to enjoy herself. After all, Chick Night is supposed to be fun for everyone!

That is why the founding members of the Hanmer chapter of Chick Night decided to include an additional regulation about the "No Guilt" rule—to lighten up the mood while making a point.

Section F, Subsection YI says the following:

> We, the founding members of Chick Night, solemnly add the following items to our list of self-care essentials: chocolate, bubble baths, flossing, more chocolate, the occasional afternoon nap, and the right to guilt-free cancellation of a Chick Night get-together. Successful integration of these new self-care essentials

will result in the well-deserved reward of self-administered chocolate.

I am pleased to report that during this time of learning, we were able to be honest with one another. That honesty led to discussions that helped us dig a little deeper into our thoughts, feelings, and beliefs so that we could better understand ourselves. Armed with that new understanding, we were able to support and encourage one another to see self-care in a new light—free of the guilt we had associated with it.

Forming Your Own Inner Circle

This may sound like I'm contradicting myself, but I really must point out that *sometimes* feelings of guilt can be powerful motivators to change unseemly behaviour and practices. Guilt does serve a purpose—but only if you are *actually guilty* of something. This is where it can get tricky. How do you know *for sure* when you should feel guilty? Some things are obvious, such as breaking the confidentiality clause or lying to a friend in an effort to avoid an uncomfortable conversation, but what about those situations where you automatically feel guilty about what you're doing and you're not even quite sure *why* you feel guilty?

Be forewarned that this dilemma may surface as you begin to form your Chick Night friendships. While you are concentrating on bonding as a group, you may also discover that individual friendships between one or more members of your chapter of Chick Night also start to form. Please let me be clear on this: *there is nothing wrong with making a one-on-one connection with one of your Chicks*. It does not mean you are being disloyal to the group, and it is not a sign that you are dishonouring the other Chicks.

I am convinced that this potential guilt trigger stems from slightly twisted logic when it comes to the issue of loyalty—in particular, loyalty to the group. That's why I wanted to address this specific guilt pitfall right now.

I've talked to countless women who have felt instant pangs of guilt because they've started socializing and connecting with one of the women in their group apart from their regular Chick Night get-togethers. My response to this has always been "Why are you choosing to feel guilty about this?" The pure joy of Chick Night is in forming relationships with women for your mutual benefit. Having some of these relationships become stronger and deeper outside of your regular group get-togethers is not a negative reflection on the group as a whole. Chick Night was never meant to be a "package deal," where you socialize with either everyone in your group or no one in your group.

In many ways, jealousy is the flip side of guilt. Instead of feeling guilty about something you did or didn't do, you may feel a pang of jealousy because of something the others did or didn't do. Jealousy can signal insecurity based on self-esteem issues or stem from a need to always be right in the middle of the action. Whatever the reason, jealousy can sometimes trip up even the most thoughtful of women.

Unless you honestly believe the group is conspiring to keep you out of the loop, it is in your best interest to remember two things: that you can't always be there and that the members of your group did not *cause* you to feel this way. When you are ready to discuss this without accusing anyone of anything, talk to your Chicks about your feelings and let them help you sort them out. Once you have identified the root cause of jealous feelings, you can let them go.

You can also begin to recognize what a blessing and relief it is that other women are around who can be there when you can't. For example, it is impossible to *always* be there the moment a friend in crisis needs you. Isn't it better to know that you have backup—that you don't have to feel guilty if you can't be with your friend in her time of need because someone else in your group can be?

I believe the pangs of guilt some women face when this happens date back to memories of childhood experiences. At some point in their past, the vast majority of women have heard the words, "If you want to be my friend, you can't be friends with her!" I call this behaviour "being grade seven." You can substitute whatever grade you were in when this first happened to you, but I bet you know what I mean by "being grade seven." Neighbourhoods and schoolyards all over the country have been witness to this form of childhood jealousy. Either we felt it ourselves or experienced it because of the attitudes of others.

Fortunately, as we've matured and grown into women, most of us have gotten over the effect of jealousy—or think we have. At this point in life, it really doesn't matter whether you were the little girl who felt jealous of the relationships other little girls formed or the one accused of disloyalty. Regardless of where you stood on the issue as a child, Chick Night can potentially trigger the memories and lingering emotions of your early experiences.

Let's take a look at this issue in the light of day and dispel any false beliefs you may have formed about loyalty once and for all. Replace them with the understanding that every relationship we form during our lifetime is a gift. Each one is meant to teach us something about ourselves. Granted, we don't always like what it shows us, but it is always something we were meant to see.

When we allow our misconceptions about group loyalty to interfere with the natural progression of individual relationships, we cheat ourselves and others out of the opportunity for important life lessons. By allowing each new relationship to evolve naturally, we gain maximum benefit and enjoyment of all our friendships. We also learn more about ourselves and can then contribute that knowledge and understanding to our Chick Night group as a whole. It's truly a win-win scenario!

Now, isn't that better than feeling guilty?

Chick Night™ Rule #9: Keep It Real

(Leave your masks at the door.)

On average, how much of your day is spent in meaningless surface chitchat? I'm referring to full conversations revolving around trivial issues that include the weather, local traffic conditions, and so on. These verbal interactions may happen with your family members, neighbours, people at work, or while you're running errands before heading home. *Where* they happen doesn't matter, but *how often* they happen does.

There is something very isolating about conversations that seem to have no meaning. They are done by remote control. This is not communication in the true sense of the word, because the two people involved are simply filling in the blanks with the appropriate comments. In reality, neither person is really listening nor being heard.

Although I recognize that idle chitchat is considered polite form in our culture, it is not something I thrive on. I have nothing against being polite (and I'm quite sure by now you have figured out that I have nothing against talking). It's just that we spend so much of our time asking people, "How are you doing?" and hearing the correct response, "Fine, thank you, and how are you?" that we aren't *really* talking to them.

These types of conversations can feel like going through the motions for nothing. It's no wonder people complain about being in a room filled with other people and feeling completely alone.

Physical proximity is no guarantee of a connection.

If you don't believe me, start paying attention to the number of people in your life who you have actual conversations with. I mean moments when you are really talking to each other about what you think or how you feel. When you begin to pay attention to your conversations, you may discover that even some lifelong relationships are not as deep and meaningful as you assumed they were.

Getting Real

When you *do* have the opportunity for real conversation, don't waste it. Chick Night is not the time to mingle, exchange "Hollywood kisses," and promise that "my people will call your people." Once you have reached a sufficient comfort level with these women, you can begin to build trust by letting your guard down more and more. It is important that you do this, because hiding behind the mask of your various roles will only slow down the process. It is up to you to relax and set aside all pretenses for a few hours. This requires a commitment on your part and involves similar commitments from the other ladies. Either you are comfortable enough to be yourself around these women or you are not. If you are not, then you need to choose different women to have Chick Night with.

Having said that, I caution you against making snap judgments about whom to invite or whom to keep in your circle of friends. Sometimes elements of annoyance can be misinterpreted as a signal from your intuition. We all have at least one girlfriend who is (how shall I put this?) "listening challenged." You know the one I mean. This woman is completely in love with the sound of her own voice. Or is she? There are a couple of possible explanations that you might want to consider before making any final decisions. She may find silence uncomfortable and therefore have a habit of jumping in to fill those momentary gaps that occur in natural conversation. Or she may simply be reacting (overly enthusiastically) to the fact that someone is actually listening to her. Can you honestly tell me that you have never been so lonely that you became a complete babbling idiot whenever anyone said hello to you? I am willing to admit to that.

So, before you eliminate your "Chatty Cathy" girlfriend as a potential Chick, I recommend that you give her a chance. She may simply need a friend who is willing to give her some direction. May I be so bold as to suggest that you use a small box of chocolates (or any other symbol you feel would be appropriate) as a "teaching tool"? As each woman has her turn sharing, she holds the chocolates. When she is finished, she passes the box to the next woman who wants to speak. The rule is that only the woman holding the chocolates is allowed to talk.

Any woman who has a natural tendency to interrupt with her own comments or story will have a visual reminder to wait her turn. It also works when this particular woman is speaking. If she has been talking for a long time with no sign of stopping to allow someone else a turn, you can offer her a gentle reminder. Try humour. You can say something like, "Hey, girlfriend, you're hogging all the chocolate."

It won't take long for her to get an inner sense of what balanced participation in a sharing conversation feels like. Consider it your gift to her.

Being Real

There are two ways to hide the real you from the world. One way is to perfect the art of avoidance by sticking to superficial conversations that don't reveal anything about your personal life or how you think or feel. The other way is by hiding behind masks—the "faces" of your various personal and professional roles.

I can tell you from experience that stripping away the protective layers provided by these faces may not be as easy as you expect. I *thought* it would be simple to drop my masks, but I was wrong. Ultimately, it will come down to how long you have been hiding behind those roles and how prepared you are to expose the real you.

The first few Chick Nights are probably going to be relatively light evenings. You will all need some time to get to know each other better. Even at this early stage, make sure to "keep it real." You don't have to share your most intimate secrets (and you may never choose to do so), but you can certainly be yourself right from the start.

Chick Night is your chance to be who you really are. Let down that guarded front of yours and have fun. Allow your sense of humour to emerge. Encourage your sense of adventure to surface. Explore new ways of seeing and thinking about the world around you. Share your thoughts and ideas with women who are equally enthusiastic about sharing theirs.

The camaraderie will develop at its own pace. If each of you allows yourself the freedom to be who you really are, the friendships will begin to take shape naturally. Meanwhile, this is your chance to let your hair down. You don't have to play *any* role. You're not "on duty," so there's no one else you have to take care of. On Chick Night you are not a wife or a mother. You are not single or married. You are not a teacher or a doctor or a store clerk or a local politician (or however else you are known in your community circles). You are just *you*.

It is highly unlikely that the other founding members will ever say, "I didn't expect you to say that or think that or act that way." They won't because they don't want to hear you say it to them! Chick Night is a safe place to be yourself.

The Hanmer chapter of Chick Night regulations Section H, Subsection I reads as follows:

> All founding members of Chick Night shall be encouraged to present a true and honest representation of personality and character, and will be supported by the other members in this. Members will practice acknowledging, to themselves and to each other, their own worth and value. Through mutual respect and self-respect, said members will work together to achieve their common goal of self-expression.

When it comes to this particular Chick Night essential, I pass the pen to Bonnie. She has lived and learned this one right before our eyes:

Keeping It Real

by Bonnie Paquette

I live and work in a rather small community. I am a teacher and have been at the same school for many years. Some of my first students are now having children. It hardly seems possible, but alas, it is true!

Living and teaching in the same community has many wonderful benefits, but it does create some privacy problems. I am someone who enjoys her privacy. I like to be able to run down to the grocery store for milk, grab a sub at the restaurant, or pick up a greeting card at the drugstore and do it anonymously. That rarely happens. Inevitably, wherever I go, I run into someone I know. Almost always, that someone is a current or former student or parent of a student.

When we first started Chick Night, my fellow Chicks were a wee bit annoyed with me. They'd turn to me, after I'd once again been spotted in a crowd, and say, "Isn't there anywhere we can take you that you won't be recognized?"

You have to realize that the whole purpose of Chick Night is to get you away from whatever you need to get away *from*. For me, it was the responsibilities of being a mother and teacher. My fellow Chicks felt obligated to shelter me the best they could from those responsibilities. They made sure school was not a topic we dwelt on (even though our sons were close in age). They could control that, but for all their trying they could not prevent the teacher from being spotted. I appreciate them all the more for trying!

Perhaps because of all that, I found it difficult (at first) to be real at Chick Night. It wasn't that I was wearing a mask. I simply had to know that my fellow Chicks were true to our confidentiality clause. Most of all, I needed the reassurance that I didn't have to keep up my teacher image.

Through my Chick Night friends' persistence, devotion and integrity, I learned I could be me. Not Bonnie the mom or Bonnie the teacher—just Bonnie. I could let down my guard and feel what I wanted, say what I wanted, and be who I wanted to be. Chick Night offers you a sanctuary where masks and former identities are checked in at the door.

Chick Night is much more than a monthly assurance of an evening out with the girls. It's the beginning of a reawakening for you. Getting out of the house for a few hours is just a perk. Beginning to thrive is the *main event*!

Chick Night™ Rule #10: Never Pass Up a Chance to Have Fun

(Fun is the answer. Do you need a question?)

When asked to describe themselves, most women will tell you what they do for a living.

The answer might be "I'm an associate dean at the university, I represent the institution at conferences all over the country, and I've been looking in on my mother ever since we moved her from her home to her apartment in the new seniors' residence."

Or they may rattle off a list that includes the following: "I'm a wife and mother of [however many] children, I'm the executive assistant to the general manager, I take my turn with carpools for dance classes, hockey, and band practices on the weekends, and I'm in charge of registration for summer baseball."

Or the list may sound more like this: "Now that my children have grown up and moved away, I'm filling the time when I'm not at work by being involved in my church and doing volunteer work in the community three evenings a week."

When each of these women is asked what she's "into" or what she likes to do, she will most likely greet the question with a pause and a blank stare. She may eventually respond with something like "Well, I was in a couple of local live theatre productions and I used to take yoga … but that was a long time ago."

I'm here to tell you something important. Your personal life does not have to be over. It didn't end; you just chose to shelve it for a while. It's time to take your life down from shelf, dust it off, and start living it again!

Participating in Chick Night is the perfect way to help you gently reestablish your connection with the world around you. This is accomplished with the help of your friends (who are also reconnecting), with chocolate (by far the most worthwhile invention in the history of the human race), and with fun (a learning tool with unlimited potential).

Fun Is Not a Four-Letter Word

I'm not quite sure why having fun has earned such a bad reputation—as if it were an unmistakable sign of irresponsible behaviour. Somewhere along the line, most of us start to believe that fun is something children have and adults leave behind as they grow up. We replace spontaneous play with scheduled tasks. We stop following the path of our imaginations in favour of more serious pursuits. Then, we pride ourselves on acting more mature. No wonder Peter Pan didn't want to grow up!

Never underestimate the value of having fun. It is the quickest way to lighten your spirit and reanimate your soul. It's also a wonderful indicator of your interests—which, if followed, may lead to hobbies and pastimes. Notice the things you have fun doing. They will help you remember those long-forgotten interests.

If your idea of having fun means drawing or painting, dig out your old arts-and-crafts supplies and set up a makeshift studio at your kitchen table for your next Chick Night. Then, think about enrolling in a local art class.

If your idea of having fun means dancing, crank up the stereo and invite the girls over for a Chick Night of dancing around your living room. Then, look for some dance classes in your area.

If your idea of having fun involves taking pictures (of people, architecture, animals, or nature), suggest that the ladies bring their cameras to your next Chick Night. Then, take an online photography course or enroll in a class at night school.

If your idea of having fun involves water fights with the garden hose, it may be an indicator that it is time for you to stop taking everything in your life quite so seriously. Lighten up your attitude and you lighten your load.

Pay attention to changes in your sense of humour. Once you begin to spend high-quality time with your Chick Night Chicks, the "knock-knock" jokes you entertain your children with are not going to cut it. Your original (pre-motherhood) sense of humour will begin to surface. It will, in fact, sense that it is time to come out and play. Watch out, though. You may discover that you actually *like* playing with water pistols, or using sidewalk chalk, or skipping rope "double Dutch," or painting each other's nails.

Remember, anything that makes you laugh is fun—no matter how silly or ridiculous or undignified it seems. There is no safer environment to try these things than during Chick Night. When it comes to this form of self-discovery, you do not have to make the journey alone. All Chick Night Chicks are free to make suggestions. This way, you may get the chance to try something you might never have thought of.

If this task sounds too daunting, please refer to Section L, Subsection OL of the Hanmer chapter of Chick Night regulations:

> We, the founding members of the Hanmer chapter of Chick Night, hereby dedicate ourselves to the pursuit of fun. We promise to explore any suggestions or whims (the more whimsical the better) put forth by any member. We also pledge to encourage all forms of silliness in our quest for the Holy Grail of Humour ... *laughter.*

May the sweet sounds of success ring in the ears of you and your Chick Night cofounders for many years to come!

While you are preparing for your well-deserved success in the area of fun, I would like to introduce you to Jessica, a young friend whom I "adopted" as an honourary daughter several years ago. She is full of life, love, and enthusiasm:

Up with Fun

by Jessica Natale

Two months shy of my twenty-third birthday, I had still never dyed my hair. I had never handed in an assignment late, never missed curfew, never had a late fee at Blockbuster, and never chosen fun over responsibility. It was time for a change!

Two months before I turned twenty-three and entered the age that for years I associated with "real" adulthood, I dyed my light brown hair a deep, dark red. While this manic makeover may resemble an identity crisis that many women face after breakups or other stressful moments, mine was more of an identity rebellion that occurred about ten years too late.

I started listening to my responses to opportunities to try new things, and I realized that I had become a slave to responsibility.

I had been saying no to practically every opportunity for new kinds of fun because of my duty as daughter, sister, babysitter, role model, teacher, etc., etc. My no's were immediate when offered new opportunities, such as motorcycle rides, concert tickets, and all-night, girls-only nights simply because I had an overwhelming sense of duty and responsibility to other people.

It seemed easier to stick to the fun that I knew let me fill my roles perfectly than to engage in new kinds of fun that would bend the borders of the identity-mould of each one of my assigned titles.

Upon further reflection, I came to understand that people are constantly defined by their roles in life. I had let other people's understanding of my roles take over—to the point where I said no before even hearing them out, before even considering that there was a new kind of fun to be had.

Taking a look around me, I am amazed at how titles define every single one of us. Mother, father, teacher, priest, lawyer, garbage collector—all these roles are accompanied by varying amounts of responsibility.

We try to fit so much into these roles that we actually forget to have fun. Though I enjoyed high school and university, I passed up almost every opportunity that I thought did not fall into the categories set up by my perceived roles in life.

Indeed, this is a personal flaw (as I see it), to have missed out on so much fun and personal growth. I hope that now that I have pinpointed the problem, I can fix it.

At twenty-three years of age, I have acquired only a handful of roles to play. Their number will increase steadily with my age as I begin to take more responsibility for different people. I worry that titles, such as wife and mother, will again force me into the no pattern I entered in my early teen years.

The cure is easy. Instead of playing the martyr and saying no (which, surprisingly, comes more easily than most moms believe) to new opportunities, the key is allowing yourself to have fun in new ways, or even fun at all!

It keeps us young and glowing inwardly and outwardly. All that research on happy endorphins must be true; there is nothing like waking up after a night spent laughing with girlfriends till the wee hours of the morning.

Make time for fun.

In this world of mass-media domination it is easy to lose who we are in titles, roles, and characters. Having fun brings us back to who we are and reminds us that there is more to our fabulous selves than just a bunch of titles.

Since my revelation, I have been saying yes! to new things (without shirking my responsibilities—there is a line, of course, and I still have a perfect record at Blockbuster).

I went on a motorcycle ride and took in three concerts. I have been less obsessively punctual, and I take time to appreciate the beautiful things that we often pass by.

There is a whole lot of fun to be had out there; we need to embrace it and spread it around! Fun shouldn't seem like work.

And for the record, as a new redhead, I am fairly certain *we* have the most fun. Do you care to take that challenge?

Jessica has figured out something it took me nearly twenty extra years to realize fully. Now that you have come to grips with two major lessons, remembering number ten will help you remember that *you* are number one.

Reasons to Be Grateful
for Chick Night™

My Top Five Countdown

Wrapping Up the Gifts for Which I Am Grateful

Well, there you have it, ladies—the Ten to Remember. The ten rules outlined in this book were created (with the aid of chocolate) over a period of nearly ten years, as a way for Bonnie, Collette, and me to gain the maximum benefit of Chick Night. Each time we encountered a challenge that might affect our ability to meet once a month, we created a new rule that eliminated that so-called challenge before one or all of us could start using it as an excuse to cancel out of our evening.

The longer we got together, the easier it became to maintain this once-a-month commitment. It's like any new habit or practice: do it long enough and it becomes a natural part of your life.

I'm so very, very glad we did! My life is happier and richer, thanks to the bond of friendship we have developed and continue to share. I am truly grateful for all the benefits of Chick Night. For me, the list of these benefits is wonderfully, blessedly long. I can assure you that the list will be just as long, if not longer, for you.

#5: The Reminder That It's Good to Be a Woman

If you've ever gotten caught up in the whole "I wish I weren't a woman" mind-set (and most of us have fallen into that trap at one time or another in our lives), you have focussed a lot of your energy on distancing yourself from things you consider "female." When *woman* becomes synonymous with *weak*, there is sometimes a subconscious tendency to eliminate traits, interests, and desires that seem gender specific.

I'm speaking from experience here. There was a long period in my life when I chose to wear pants instead of dresses. I avoided love songs like the plague. I ignored fiction novels centred on relationships in favour of spy novels. Does any of this sound familiar to you? If not, good for you. If it does, there is something I want to say to you. It took me a long time to realize that rather than continually running from who and what I am, it made far more sense to notice and appreciate my inner strengths and potential.

Can you imagine how much easier this initial thought process would have been to integrate if I had already been a member of a chapter of Chick Night?

Reconnecting with women on a monthly basis will help you see yourself as a member of a truly remarkable gender. Recognizing the character traits and personality pluses of the women in your Chick Night chapter will help you spot your own strengths and attributes. If that isn't enough, you can be guaranteed that the women around you will point out aspects about you that they respect and admire.

As Helen Reddy began proudly proclaiming in the 1970s, "I am woman, hear me roar." I wonder if she is a member of a chapter of Chick Night. If not, she is certainly welcome to join ours!

#4: The Reminder That You Are Not Alone

I have never been able to figure out why women insist on believing that whatever challenges they are facing in life are unique to them. How many times have you dealt with something for days, weeks, months, or even years all alone—only to discover long after the fact that at least three of your neighbours, friends, or coworkers went through the very same thing?

Each time this happens, do you say to yourself, "Next time, I'll talk to somebody about this"? Now, based on previous personal experience, let me guess what you actually do the next time. You suffer in silence … again!

As of right now, this very minute, I want you to think of this habit as more detrimental than smoking, more disgusting than flossing your teeth at a vegetable stand, and more dangerous than hang gliding nude over a cactus farm. This is a habit you simply must kick, once and for all. For the sake of your mental and emotional well being, and for your self-esteem, I sincerely urge you to drop the belief that no one else has ever gone through what you are going through right now.

Here's why:

- You are needlessly increasing the intensity of your inner turmoil.
- You are convincing yourself that *you* are the problem.
- You are prolonging the failure to resolve this issue.
- You are robbing yourself of valuable guidance and advice.
- You are lying to yourself.

You are not alone!

There are women in your life who have already dealt with—or are dealing with—exactly the same issues you are now facing. The scenario may be different, but the fundamental issue is the same.

This is one of the basic aspects of Chick Night. Something about seeing the same small, trusted group of women each month fosters not only a level of understanding but also a unique perspective on each other. If something is bothering you, these women will sense it. Believe me. You can try blowing it off with a resigned shrug, but they will know.

This instinctive "knowing" does not mean that your fellow Chicks will automatically pry into areas you are unprepared or unwilling to share. There may be times that you truly are not ready to talk about what is bothering you. In that case, your fellow Chicks will most likely smile knowingly and say, "Okay, when you feel like talking about it, we'll be here."

Sometimes that is all it takes. That first moment when you remember that you are not alone brings with it a powerful emotional wave of comfort. Other times, that initial jolt of reality is like having a door gently swing open when you've been wishing for quite a while that someone would just come over and kick the blasted thing down.

Regardless of your reaction (and it will most likely be based on how long you have been dealing with your current dilemma), knowing you are surrounded by people who care and who really do understand what you are going through is worth more than a zero balance on every single one of your credit cards.

I am incredibly grateful to my Chicks for their willingness to listen, to understand, to share my burdens, and to remind me that I am not alone. Neither are you!

#3: The Nourishing Bond

Over time, a nourishing bond develops between the women in a chapter of Chick Night.

We are each other's battery charger. We provide a safe, loving cocoon where physically, mentally, emotionally, and yes, sometimes even spiritually exhausted women can relax, regroup, and recharge.

This is another element of Chick Night. No matter how tired or drained I feel while getting ready to head out the door for Chick Night, I know I will feel better upon my return.

I say this with unbounded optimism balanced by practical experience. Chick Night is not an instant fix for everything. However, it does offer an immediate benefit that you can't get from an ordinary night out. The difference comes from the comforting blanket of friendship you can snuggle under while you reconnect with your Chicks.

If you are feeling like someone pulled the plug on your energy, going out for Chick Night is a highly effective way to replenish your reserves. Instead of working until you're exhausted and flopping into bed with the knowledge that you'll have to start all over again tomorrow, do something for yourself tonight! It doesn't have to be fancy or expensive or complicated as long as it's with your Chicks.

Remember that one of the main rules of Chick Night deals

with temporarily shedding your life roles (girlfriend, wife, mother, grandmother, career woman, stay-at-home mom) in favour of reconnecting with yourself. When you strip off the roles, you momentarily drop the weight of the responsibilities. You only have to think about you. You only have to answer to you. You only have to do for you during Chick Night.

Doesn't that sound like a welcome break? It's a great opportunity for a stop-the-world-and-let-me-off moment. Once this wonderful feeling has set in, you can start enjoying yourself.

(Warning: The more exhausted and drained you are, the more radical this idea may seem. Stick with it, though. You'll discover it's not quite as foreign a concept as you originally thought.)

I have polled my Chicks. All three of us confirm that we feel deep and definite gratitude for the nourishing bond we have created. It has been a lifeline at times. This source of comfort, security, and energy renewal has an unlimited supply. It has proved our conviction that feeling good is the right of every woman on earth!

#2: The Guaranteed Honesty

I once saw a stand-up comedienne explain the difference between men and women by using the following scenario. She asked all the men in the audience what the correct response is when a woman asks, "Does this dress make me look fat?" There was a deafening silence in the room. She then posed that same question to the women in the audience. The instant response was a resounding "No!"

I still chuckle when I think about that routine. This comedienne was playing on the ability women have to instinctively recognize when the effective delivery of a little white lie would make another woman feel better about herself.

This seems to be a trick that most women understand how, and when, to perform. I have no qualms with that. Whether or not you choose to employ this technique from time to time is completely up to you. However, the members of the Hanmer chapter of Chick Night have unanimously decided that during actual Chick Night get-togethers, we will be thoroughly, scrupulously, 100 percent honest with one another.

At first glance, this may seem a little scary, but you need to remember that being honest isn't the same as being mean. The honest answer to "Does this dress make me look fat?" could just as easily be "The first one you tried on looked nicer."

If you're still convinced that agreeing to be completely honest with each other is just asking for trouble, let's look at the built-in safety net Chick Night offers. You have handpicked the women in your chapter. You have developed a level of trust that manages to cut through all your personal and professional roles. Ground rules have already been established, so no one will pressure you to talk about things you are not ready to discuss.

When you *are* ready to talk about something important, will it be very helpful if these women simply tell you what they think you want to hear instead of what you actually need to hear? What good will *that* do you?

Do not squander these wonderful opportunities to get honest, loving feedback from women you trust! Their intentions are pure. They seek only to help you understand the bigger lesson hidden within the current situation. Chick Night can provide you with a third-person perspective when you need it most. Ultimately, whether or not you take advantage of it is your choice. The important thing is to remember that the option is there.

#1: The Power of Laughter

I honestly do not know how anyone successfully navigates through life without laughter. More important, why would anyone choose to respond to the life lessons that are most surely on their way *without* using the power of laughter?!

According to an article at helpguide.org, there are significant health benefits to laughter. It relieves muscular tension, lowers stress hormones, boosts the immune system, protects the heart, and triggers the release of endorphins to produce a general sense of well-being. In addition, laughter eases anxiety, increases feelings of joy, and enhances resilience. All this is possible by physically reacting to the presence of humour.

Any time Bonnie, Collette, and I get together, there is bound to be laughter. Even during an S.O.S. Chick Night, we eventually help the Chick in distress find something to laugh about. This may seem insensitive or sound like we choose to look only at the superficial view of the situation, but neither of those is the case. The reason laughter is always an element of Chick Night is that it is such a powerful tool. Whether in response to desperation or despair, laughter cuts through the darkness quickly and effectively.

The members of the Hanmer chapter of Chick Night believe that there are two ways to look at any situation. You can see the bad, terrible, horrible, awful, hopeless, unkind, unfair side, or you can look for the gift, blessing, silver lining, lesson, and (you guessed it) humourous side.

The "something funny" may not be absolutely hilarious, but if you look closely, with the help of your Chick friends, you will find something in the situation worth chuckling about. Better yet, try guffawing. To really be kind to yourself, start belly laughing. Let loose with the type of laughter that has you holding your sides and wiping tears off your face.

No matter what is going on in your life, you will feel better if you can find something to laugh about.

My best girlfriend from high school is a firm believer in the power of laughter. Laurie harnesses its benefits whenever possible and helps others do the same.

During my darkest days in the early months after the end of my marriage, she encouraged me to draw upon laughter as a tool for strength and an antidote for despair. No matter how long it took, she never hung up the phone without having first made me laugh. It became a joke between us, because as soon as I started to laugh, she would say, "Well, my work here is done. Bye-bye," and that would get us both laughing.

When I look back on it, the wisdom she displayed is obvious. Not only did she show me support and friendship with each phone call, but she also managed to help me *feel better* afterward. That is a gift I would like to pay forward to you!

Helping someone reconnect with her laughter is a true act of friendship. Pass this gift along to your fellow Chicks, but first, take a hearty helping of humour for yourself.

I am grateful for these five elements of Chick Night. Each one serves a unique purpose. Strung together, they create the links of a friendship chain that will support, inspire, encourage, and carry you through all the challenges and blessings, turmoil, and triumphs of your life.

The Elements of a Chick Night™ Chapter

The Chick Night™ Mandate:
Chicks of the Chocolate, Unite!

The Hanmer chapter of Chick Night regulations Section A, Subsection 1 notes the following for the record:

> It is the sworn duty of every Chick Night Chick to do your best to *remember* who you really are, what you like to do, what makes you laugh, how to have fun, and how to be spontaneous.

As you begin to remember these things, you will trigger a process of reawakening. The long-hidden, forgotten *you* will reemerge. Gradually, you will notice that you have started to expand your life as a wife and mother and career woman to include *you*. You will soon discover that you are actually a woman worth getting to know. You will also discover that you are far more interesting than you ever expected. You will become a woman who is a lot of fun to be around (and to be).

While you are learning and discovering all of this, you will be sharing the experience with other women who are coming to similar conclusions about themselves. The true strength of Chick Night is in the desire of its members to help each other. Each of us shares a fundamental desire to figure out who we are and what we want out of life. The bonds of our "chocolate sisterhood" provide a safe and supportive environment in which we can do the necessary self-exploration while also assisting and encouraging each other.

It is this inward journey that makes all the difference—enriching the quality of your life, increasing your level of self-confidence, and solidifying your inner happiness and contentment.

This phenomenon comes with an added bonus. Self-fulfilled, positive, energetic people attract the same types of people. They also attract self-fulfilling, positive, and energetic opportunities for themselves. How's *that* for a win-win situation?

Chick Night is a gift you give yourself and share with others. Enjoy!

Rules and Regulations: An Overview

As you and your friends begin to form your own local chapter of Chick Night, it might be handy to have a complete list of all the rules and regulations found in this book. The following pages can act as a reference guide for you to follow.

Chick Night™ Rules: The Ten to Remember

1: All Chick Nights Must Involve Chocolate.
2: Chick Night Must Happen a Minimum of Once a Month.
3: No Children Allowed.
4: Nothing Complicated.
5: Keep the Numbers Down.
6: Don't Let Money Be an Issue.
7: The Confidentiality Clause.
8: Never Do Guilt about Chick Night.
9: Keep It Real.
#10: Never Pass Up a Chance to Have Fun.

Hanmer Chapter of Chick Night™ Regulations

Section A, Subsection 1:

It is the sworn duty of every Chick Night Chick to do your best to *remember* who you really are, what you like to do, what makes you laugh, how to have fun, and how to be spontaneous.

Section A, Subsection OK (in a friendly, singsong voice):

Attention, ladies. This evening's presentation of Chick Night is about to begin. Please turn off all cell phones and electronic devices to eliminate the possibility of distractions that might detract from your full enjoyment of this evening's festivities. Your cooperation in this matter is greatly appreciated. Thank you!

Section C (for Chocolate), Subsection 2B:

After careful consideration and thoughtful discussion by all three founding members, the vote is unanimous: chocolate (in any form) consumed during the normal course of any and all Chick Nights is (now and forever) deemed calorie-free and fat-free.

Section C (for Chocolate), Subsection 3B:

Speaking with one's mouth full is permissible under the following conditions:

- The Chick's mouth is full of chocolate (which we all know deserves to be savoured and enjoyed)
- The Chick is using positive reinforcement in response to another Chick's comment.
- The Chick has just remembered a particularly motivating, funny, or empowering anecdote.
- The Chick is expressing appreciation for the love, support, and friendship of her fellow Chicks.
- The Chick's mouth is full of chocolate (this one is worth repeating).

Section Cha, Subsection Ching:

After careful consideration of all viewpoints, concerns, perceptions, facts, and fiction, it has been decided that lack of funds is not deemed relevant to the execution of Chick Night.

Section D, Subsection 3A:

All authorized chapters of Chick Night have the right to reassign, reposition, or recategorize specific calendar dates for the purpose of celebrating Chick Night.

Section F, Subsection YI:

We, the founding members of Chick Night, solemnly add the following items to our list of self-care essentials: chocolate, bubble baths, flossing, more chocolate, the occasional afternoon nap, and the right to guilt-free cancellation of a Chick Night get-together. Successful integration of these new self-care essentials will result in the well-deserved reward of self-administered chocolate.

Section G, Subsection O:

All women in attendance of an officially sanctioned Chick Night will be present in not only body, but mind and spirit as well. Said women will concentrate on themselves and their enjoyment, focussing on guilt-free pleasure. Henceforth and hereafter, all founding members of Chick Night will engage in such frivolity and merriment as is unanimously agreed upon, fully understanding the future rewards and benefits to all family members.

Section H, Subsection I:

All founding members of Chick Night shall be encouraged to present a true and honest representation of personality and character, and will be supported by the other members in this. Members will practice acknowledging, to themselves and to each other, their own worth and value. Through mutual respect and self-respect, said members will work together to achieve their common goal of self-expression.

Section L, Subsection OL:

We, the founding members of the Hanmer chapter of Chick Night, hereby dedicate ourselves to the pursuit of fun. We promise to explore any suggestions or whims (the more whimsical the better) put forth by any member. We also pledge to encourage all forms of silliness in our quest for the Holy Grail of Humour ... laughter.

Section M, Subsection E:

As a founding member of Chick Night, it is your sworn duty to uphold the basic tenets of your chapter. During the course of any and all Chick Nights, you will solemnly promise to abdicate all duties and responsibilities associated with your multitasking roles of wife and mother. You will instead concentrate solely on nurturing *you*—the woman, the person, the individual.

Section N, Subsection O:

No offspring of any member may attend a Chick Night. (N-O spells *NO!*)

Section N, Subsection X:

No new members may be invited, either verbally or through inference, without first being put to a vote. Only a unanimous verdict will result in invitation.

Section O, Subsection K:

If the logistical coordination of a Chick Night should, at any time, begin to feel so complicated that it might give one or more members the slightest inclination toward a headache, said logistical co-ordination is to be terminated immediately. Feeling stressed out about any aspect of Chick Night is strictly prohibited.

Section Q, Subsection T:

Each founding member of Chick Night has the right, and will exercise the right, to complete and total confidentiality. Nothing that is said, inferred, or alluded to over the course of any given Chick Night will be repeated (or even hinted at) without the express written permission of each and every member of said Chick Night chapter. End of discussion.

Section Y, Subsection ES:

All rules can and will be broken in the interest of a good time.

Chick-speak Glossary of Terms

Chick: a woman in pursuit of self-discovery

Chick Night: any evening that creates the opportunity to bond with other Chicks for the purpose of mutual self-discovery

Chick-speak: universal language immediately identifiable by women anywhere in the world (fortunately or unfortunately sounds like total gibberish to most men)

Chick time: any opportunity for a Chick to have fun in the company of other women

Chocolate: lifeblood of women, basic component found in female DNA (see *Estrogen*)

Chocolate Sisters: the bond between women that runs as deep as their very lifeblood, a connection that transcends all other factors

Come Unarmed: you don't need to bring any chocolate. The rest of us will come prepared. (This phrase is usually reserved for the recipient of an S.O.S. Chick Night.)

Confidentiality: I'm not telling! (Pinkie swear!)

Dessert: the only section of the meal that really matters

Diet: North American version of the infamous Chinese water torture

Essentials: absolute necessities with which to sustain life (examples: chocolate, Chick Night)

Estrogen: female hormone, directly linked to consumption of chocolate

Female Fellowship: estrogen-rich companionship that provides balance and stability through emotionally fulfilling interaction

Fun: If you need to look this one up, please read this handbook again.

Guilt: dangerous internal disorder of the thought processes; if left untreated can cause crippling side effects that limit one's ability to enjoy life (see also *Mother Guilt*)

Hoot: description of the kind of fun that can sustain you for days

Indulgence: refusing to allow any obstacles to stand in the way of your life experiences

Logistical coordinator: the woman in the group who most loves sending e-mails or talking on the phone

Mother Guilt: dormant gene activated by childbirth; symptoms can be alleviated with massive doses of estrogen (see *Estrogen*)

Pampered: any decision or action that creates enjoyment for you (the opposite of trying to please everyone else)

Spontaneous: a joyful response expressed directly from the heart without first running it past your head (where you would probably veto it)

Sweet Smorgasbord: a variety of desserts served simultaneously (and it's only polite to try everything)

Testosterone: male hormone, directly linked to the TV remote control

Whimsical: strictly for pleasure—not logical, practical, necessary, or needed

Here's the Catch:
There Is No Catch!

The only unbreakable rule of Chick Night is Section Y, Subsection ES:

> "All rules can and will be broken in the interest of a good time."

Understanding and abiding by this rule holds the key to the successful incorporation of your very own chapter of Chick Night. There are no boundaries limiting your ability to have fun. No *real* boundaries, that is. There have only ever been the limitations you have placed on yourself.

Strip away all the roadblocks and ignore all the Catch-22s. Where there is a will, there really *is* a way. Learn to be flexible and think creatively. It will open your eyes, your mind, your heart, (and even) your soul.

The lessons contained in this book are now yours to practice. The time has come for you to begin to put what you have learned into action.

There's a big beautiful world out there. Get out and explore it!

After all this time together, it's really hard for me to just say good-bye, so let's keep in touch instead. I would love to hear from you. E-mail me about your experiences starting your own Chick Night chapter, or let me know about a particularly fun evening you had with your Chicks.

Maybe we could even get some of your letters compiled with other women's letters and (who knows?) put together *anothe*r Chick Night book. In the meantime, I hope you are able to take some of the things you have learned in this handy handbook and apply them to your routine. Spice up your life a little! (Chocolate is a spice, right?)

E-mail me at colleen@mychicknight.com.
You can also post your comments and stories on my blog at www.mychicknight.com.
I hope to hear from you soon.

Yours in friendship,
Colleen